FAMILY WELLNESS SKILLS

Quick Assessment and Practical Interventions for the Mental Health Professional

Joseph L. Hernandez

A Norton Professional Book

FAMILY WELLNESS SKILLS

Quick Assessment and Practical Interventions for the Mental Health Professional

JOSEPH L. HERNANDEZ, PhD

W. W. Norton & Company
New York • London

Figures reprinted by permission of Family Wellness Associates.

For information about permission to reproduce selections from this book, write to
Permissions, W. W. Norton & Company, Inc., 500 Fifth Avenue, New York, NY 10110

For information about special discounts for bulk purchases, please contact
W. W. Norton Special Sales at specialsales@wwnorton.com or 800-233-4830

Manufacturing by Quad Graphics, Fairfield
Production manager: Leeann Graham

Library of Congress Cataloging-in-Publication Data

Hernandez, Joseph L., 1949–
Family wellness skills : quick assessment and practical interventions for
the mental health professional / Joseph L. Hernandez, PhD. — First edition.
pages ; cm
"A Norton Professional Book."
Includes bibliographical references and index.
ISBN 978-0-393-70632-1 (hardcover)
1. Mentally ill—Family relationships. 2. Families—Mental health—Handbooks, manuals,
etc. 3. Psychotherapist and patient—Handbooks, manuals, etc. I. Title.
RC455.4.F3H48 2013
616.89—dc23
2012034629

ISBN: 978-0-393-70632-1

W. W. Norton & Company, Inc., 500 Fifth Avenue, New York, N.Y. 10110
www.wwnorton.com

W. W. Norton & Company Ltd., Castle House
75/76 Wells Street, London W1T 3QT

1 2 3 4 5 6 7 8 9 0

Contents

Acknowledgments

BE CAREFUL WHAT you ask for—you may get it. On the other hand, if you don't ask you may never get. I always wanted to write a book. Now I've completed the goal, but not before an unusual amount of blood, sweat, and tears was expended on the project. I genuinely hope that readers will catch the joy of helping others, will develop strategies for becoming life-changing catalysts, and will enhance skills already in their toolbox.

I wish to thank Virginia Morgan Scott and George Doub for developing the Family Wellness model. From these excellent teachers, I caught their passion for helping people change and I learned the necessary skills to help individuals and families succeed. Another early mentor was Dr. Carlos Gonsalves, who showed me that although mental health professionals know big words, it is the small words that matter when people are under stress and need to change. Thanks also to Flo Creighton for her tireless efforts in teaching the Family Wellness model and in strengthening the curriculum and supportive materials.

I wish to thank my partners at Family Wellness Associates (Michelle Hernandez, Ana Morante, and Mike and Erin Simile) for their passion and boundless energy in seeking to change lives and communities by teaching the Family Wellness model throughout the United States and around the world. I also value their kind friendship over time. Friendship can be good medicine.

Naturally, no project of any value can be completed without a huge amount of support from the people who really matter in life. Thanks to my wife, Michelle; my son, Joel; my daughter-in-law, Kim; my grandkids, Jacob and Jessica; and my wonderful extended family, who have been on this amazing journey with me and who have always shown me love and patience.

Speaking of patience, thanks to my editor, Deborah Malmud, without whom this project would never have become a reality.

Introduction

There has to be a way to get what we know works in psychotherapy to the people who may never darken the doorway of a therapist's office.

Private communication between Carl Rogers and George Doub

THE CORE CONCEPTS and set of skills that form the foundation for this book come from an internationally known and highly respected program known as the Family Wellness model. Mental health professionals will learn the Family Wellness model, including a specific set of quick assessment skills and intervention strategies that can be integrated into almost any psychotherapist's toolbox. The Family Wellness model is not a distinct psychotherapeutic system. Instead, it is an organized way of thinking about people, families, and organizations that is strength based, intervention filled, and outcome driven. The skills identified in this model can assist professionals in quickly assessing their clients' strengths, skills, and needs. The concepts from this model can aid in treatment plan development. The treatment plan will suggest practical interventions that promise increased opportunities for success.

In efforts both to understand the human condition and to ameliorate "dis-ease," mental health professionals today utilize one or more of approximately 400 systems of psychotherapy, with varying degrees of efficacy. Clinicians have wildly differing perspectives on what makes people tick. The theoretical orientation of each therapist becomes that professional's worldview with respect to mental health. This orientation gives the clinician perspective on who the clients are, how they got that way, and what it will take for them to get better. No matter what orientation is used, the therapist can incorporate Family Wellness concepts and become even more effective in helping people.

The basic Family Wellness concepts are explored in the following chapters from the perspective of mental health professionals working in the trenches, often with people who are making life-altering decisions, and frequently in a relatively limited time during which clinicians must be effective.

The first section of this book lays out the two jobs that everyone needs to balance in becoming a healthy person: to be an individual and to connect with others. The second section outlines the three skills that individuals must practice to be healthy: speak, listen, and cooperate. The third section describes the three patterns found in healthy couples and families: maintain equal value with parents in charge; keep room to be close and apart; and expect change. The epilogue focuses on the importance of therapists practicing self-care if they are going to be of any lasting use to others.

This introduction details the history of the Family Wellness perspective and the theoretical bases for the model. It also sets the stage for how clinicians using the Family Wellness model can view the major tasks of the psychotherapeutic or people-helping endeavor: assessment, treatment planning, and practical intervention.

HISTORY

The Family Wellness model was developed in 1980 by Virginia Morgan Scott and George Doub.

Virginia Morgan Scott is a licensed clinical social worker who developed the undergraduate schools of social work at the University of Pittsburgh and at San Jose State University, and also taught at San Francisco State University. Virginia underwent extensive postgraduate training in family therapy, systems, Gestalt, and change theories. Her social work training took her to Pennsylvania, where she trained under Salvador Minuchin in his work on structural family therapy at the Philadelphia Child Guidance Clinic. Virginia returned home to Santa Cruz, California, convinced that the concepts being developed in family therapy could be taught, not just experienced in the rarefied environment of a therapist's office. Having over a decade of teaching experience, Virginia provided extensive social work training for new therapists and supervision and consultation for experienced clinicians. Her natural professional inclination was toward obtaining an academic understanding of important issues such as power differentials and the relationship of interacting individuals. Her clinical work focused on helping children, adolescents, and adults work through relationship issues and the emotional sequelae of physical, emotional, and sexual abuse. The desire of Virginia's heart was to expend energy on prevention rather than on damage control after the fact.

George Doub was a former parish priest, a licensed marriage and family therapist, and a community organizer with a special concern for people from various cultures. He founded Alum Rock Counseling Center in San Jose, California, which is a crisis agency working with at-risk youth (dealing with alcohol, drugs, and school failure), runaway adolescents, and fragile families. Through his spiritual parish work, his psychotherapeutic training, and his organizational acumen, George was able to forge coalitions of individuals, agencies, and entities on behalf of underserved populations. With his boundless energy, visionary prowess, and charismatic communication style, George engaged school systems in working together with his counseling agency on programs involving truancy abatement. He convinced police departments to direct juveniles to counseling instead of juvenile hall in efforts at burglary suppression. He worked with the courts and social service agencies in developing programs to protect children from physical abuse, sexual abuse, and neglect. George was actively involved throughout his life in community efforts to improve the lives of individuals, families, and organizations. In these efforts, George crossed paths and worked with individuals such as Cesar Chavez, Carl Rogers, and Virginia Satir.

Dr. Josette Mondanaro, a physician, was director of the California State Department of Drug Abuse Prevention. Her clinic in Santa Cruz, Wingspread, worked with drug-addicted families. Dr. Mondanaro asked Virginia Morgan Scott and George Doub to develop a psychoeducational program that would assist the entire family in ameliorating severe dysfunction and would help prevent future family problems. Dr. Mondanaro wanted therapeutic outcomes from an educational model, with an emphasis on prevention rather than palliative treatment. She was frustrated by the fact that children with physical and emotional problems that were caused by the parents' substance abuse returned to the family systems that produced the problems in the first place. This vicious cycle produced adolescents who continued in their parents' footsteps and procreated new patients for Dr. Mondanaro to treat. This was a job she did not want.

Virginia Morgan Scott and George Doub recognized that the people with the greatest need for therapeutic interventions were often the least likely to seek them out. In the best-case scenarios, these individuals would participate in treatment programs only when ordered by the court and only after severe damage had already been done to themselves or to their families.

One of the inspirations for the Family Wellness model was a conversation between George Doub and the eminent psychotherapist Carl Rogers at a conference in San Diego, California. Carl Rogers lamented that many wonderful advances had been made by psychotherapists, who used their training and skills exclusively in the service of people who came to their offices. Professional psychotherapists were going through increasingly arduous training programs and providing excellent services, but mostly in the privacy of their offices. Those seeking treatment tended to be white upper- and middle-class individuals and families. Carl Rogers wondered together with George if there was any way of translating the increasingly complex therapeutic jargon into everyday language that would be more understandable to people of any socioeconomic status and ethnic or cultural background.

Carl Rogers told George Doub that he believed psychotherapists needed to find ways of taking the concepts, techniques, and skills out of the psychotherapy office and into the community if they were ever to make a significant difference in culturally divergent communities.

Virginia Morgan Scott and George Doub began developing the Family Wellness model in 1980 with the understanding that many people who need help will never enter the office of a psychotherapist. They also came to believe that some people will not persevere in treatment because they do not understand or believe in psychotherapy and because of lack of money to pay for services, lack of providers in some areas, language barriers, or cultural insensitivity to the needs of certain people on the part of some treatment providers. They also realized that there could never be enough therapists to meet the ever-increasing demand for services.

Virginia and George borrowed the best concepts from the social sciences regarding personal and interpersonal functioning and translated them into everyday language. They proposed to train the natural leaders in various ethnic communities to become Family Wellness instructors who would then lead community-based psychoeducation classes on marriage and family life. George and Virginia believed that by training people who were identified as community leaders to provide educational resources to the people, the dual goals of treatment and prevention could be accomplished. They believed that this model would be a cost-effective method of expanding advances in the social sciences out of the university ivory towers and private practice offices and into the homes of those in great need. They obtained money from a State of California Drug and Alcohol Abuse Prevention grant, and from the David and Lucile Packard Foundation, the Luke B. Hancock Foundation, the Walter S. Johnson Foundation, United Way, the Children's Trust Fund, the Santa Clara County Child Abuse Prevention Program, and other nonprofit entities for this endeavor.

Family Wellness draws from a variety of psychotherapeutic systems, including dynamic, cognitive, behavioral, communication, change, and systemic theories. This model is uniquely shaped to help psychotherapists develop or enhance skills for working with individuals, couples, and families because its theoretical underpinnings resonate with most mainstream people helpers. Family Wellness is not simply another system of psychological or psychosocial theory. Instead, it is a coherent psychoeducational model that can be used by practitioners of divergent psychotherapeutic orientations. Family Wellness provides a map for quick assessment, treatment plan development, and practical intervention.

Since its inception in 1980, over 1,000,000 people have attended Family Wellness classes and workshops worldwide. Well over 10,000 people have been trained in the Family Wellness curriculum to become instructors of the model. Many psychotherapists have incorporated Family Wellness training into their clinical work. The wide appeal of this model stems from its ability to translate complex theories of psychopathology, developmental issues, change theory, and family functioning into everyday language that makes sense, especially in times of crisis. It is strength based, focuses on skills and behavioral change, and has been shown to be effective with a variety of cultures within the United States and around the world.

THEORETICAL UNDERPINNINGS

It is a mistake to believe that the Family Wellness model is atheoretical. In fact, the model is deeply rooted in psychosocial theory. The model was created not to repudiate theoretical understanding but to translate complex psychosocial theory into understandable everyday language. Family Wellness attempts to make the complex simple without becoming simplistic. The idea is to communicate the wealth of psychosocial theory in such a way that people who might not otherwise benefit from formal psychotherapy can benefit from the art and science of the psychotherapeutic endeavor.

Every psychotherapist has his or her own conceptualization of why people are the way they are, why they behave the way they do, and what it takes for people to become ill, dysfunctional, or inauthentic. Similarly, each mental health professional has an idea of what it takes for people to get better, do well, or achieve their potential. The therapeutic orientation of every clinician forms the basis for his or her therapeutic worldview and provides the guide for assessment, treatment planning, and intervention. The Family Wellness model has never sought to become yet another school of psychotherapy. Instead, Family Wellness seeks to translate complex thought from existing psychosocial theory into direct and everyday language that becomes accessible when people need it the most: when they are in crisis.

In modern Western thought, individual theories of understanding humans in the social sciences generally reference Sigmund Freud, Carl Jung, and Alfred Adler. As the reader will see in the following chapters, there is nothing within the Family Wellness model that contraindicates its use in the therapy office regardless of which of these "big three" psychotherapeutic traditions one adheres to. Family Wellness has a strong affinity with Adlerian thought due to Adler's emphasis on the importance of education in helping develop improved personal and interpersonal functioning.

Developmental theories in the social sciences focus on various aspects of being human, including psychosexual stages (Freud), psychosocial stages (Erik Erikson), cognitive capacity (Piaget), or moral reasoning (Kohlberg). Again, the Family Wellness model does not preclude a worldview based on any of the major developmental theorists. In fact, a great deal of time is spent in classroom work and in the therapeutic endeavor helping people understand the stage of development in which they find themselves and the tasks that are required to successfully maneuver through these stages. Successful treatment gives clients a road map of where they have been in the various stages of development and of where they are going. It also gives them skills for successfully maneuvering the journey.

Change theory forms one of the crucial aspects of the Family Wellness model. Change is required for individuals to progress through the developmental stages. When people do not change, they get stuck. The process of helping people is to help them get "unstuck." This is similar to the concept of the therapeutic endeavor described by Irvin Yalom as "obstruction removal." The primary theoretical underpinning related to change for Family Wellness comes from the work of Virginia Satir.

Behavioral theorists teach us about learning, why and how people change, and the importance of antecedents, behaviors, and consequences for being human. Learning theorists like Pavlov, Skinner, and others have focused on change from a behavioral perspective. Other theorists have focused on change from a cognitive perspective. Family Wellness melds the two methods of conceptualizing how people change by finding practical ways to shift people's intentions into actions. Family Wellness practitioners ask people, "What are you going to do?" They do not ask, "What are you going to try?" Family Wellness usually asks, "What did you notice?" rather than "How did you feel?" Wellness practitioners emphasize the importance of behavioral and attitudinal change.

Family systems theorists such as Gregory Bateson, Bowen, and others emphasize the interrelatedness of family members, including how families tend to organize and understand each person's role within the family. Minuchin's structural family therapy highlights the importance of hierarchy in forming healthy families, boundaries, and the subsystems that develop within families. Carter and McGoldrick describe the changes that families undergo when upheaval occurs in the familial status quo. In systems theory, whatever anyone does in a family affects everyone else within that family. All of these concepts are foundational to how Family Wellness practitioners assist individuals and families to organize themselves and to work toward change. Wellness helps clients recognize that while they cannot change others, their own changes greatly affect others. The best hope of having others change is to change ourselves.

In summary, the Family Wellness model draws from a wealth of psychological and psychosocial theory and translates that theory into everyday language. This book is designed to benefit the mental health professional by highlighting the primary tenets of the Family Wellness model and by showing the value of the model in the assessment of individuals, in treatment planning, and in practical interventions that can be implemented within the therapeutic environment.

The reader of this book will learn new ways of looking at old problems through the lens of what is working rather than through the traditional medical model of dysfunction. The therapist who utilizes the Family Wellness model will begin to catch people doing something right rather than looking for what they are doing wrong. By looking at people's strengths and by developing treatment plans that include practical interventions for change, the mental health professional will likely experience increased success and satisfaction in the science and art that is psychotherapy.

FAMILY WELLNESS SKILLS

Quick Assessment and Practical Interventions
for the Mental Health Professional

SECTION I

TWO JOBS

1

Be an Individual

The Importance of Being Me

UNIQUE AS A snowflake or a fingerprint: each of us is like no other. We are individually the product of our history and that history cannot possibly be replicated. William James developed an early perspective on the self. He posited two elements of self-theory, the "Me" and the "I." The Me is the self as object, the self one can describe based on physical characteristics, personality traits, social relationships, thoughts, and feelings. The I is the sum of a capacity for agency or initiation of behaviors; a sense of uniqueness, a sense of continuity, and an awareness of one's own awareness.

Discussions among mental health professionals about being an individual generally include concepts such as self-esteem and self-confidence. Being an emotionally healthy individual ideally flows from developing and sustaining a realistic and positive sense of self. Individuals assess their own strengths and limitations predominantly in response to how they believe others view them, especially in the early years of life. Appraisals about the self begin at birth, become part of the subconscious based on perceptions of the reactions and responses of care providers, and are seared into conscious experience based on the interpersonal relationships that are experienced by the time children reach the first years of school.

The experiences in each stage of life after the early formative years either confirm and cement an individual's sense of self or cause the person to reevaluate the self. The more negative the early sense of self, the harder it

3

can be to disavow that perception, even in the face of contradictory evidence. When individuals receive messages that are not consonant with internalized beliefs about self (cognitive dissonance), they will shoot either the message or the messenger. It is hard to receive positive messages about ourselves when we are convinced that we are not valuable. Interestingly, it seems that when the early messages about self are extremely positive, we are not as easily dissuaded from our positive perceptions of self by contradictory negative messages.

When psychotherapists discuss what it means to be an individual, they are usually talking about personality. Personality is the essence of who we are, what makes us tick, what causes us to act the way we do, why we think the way we do, and what it is to be who and what we are. Over time, psychotherapists have developed a variety of typologies regarding what it means to be Me. Each construct of personality has developed from particular psychotherapeutic worldviews that serve as the foundation for that perspective. Figure 1.1 shows some popular differing perspectives on what it means to be uniquely Me.

Each mental health professional decides what it means to be an individual, to be a self, to be Me. That determination is guided by the clinician's theoretical orientation. The same framework is used to define which factors prevent or enhance the healthy development of the individual. These beliefs guide the therapist in purpose and practice.

A healthy sense of self allows people to appreciate and enjoy their basic worth and value as humans. Realistic and positive self-esteem also forms the foundation for individuals to speak up in social interactions and to have the best chance of meeting their needs. A strong sense of self suggests, and is often associated with, leadership skills and general success in life.

For individuals who are without a realistic and positive sense of self, stressors and psychopathological manifestations tend to develop due to personal and interpersonal difficulties. People become discouraged, depressed, and anxious when seeing themselves as inadequate or incomplete. Such perceived inadequacies may result in intrapsychic and interpersonal conflicts that are difficult to resolve. Individuals with an inadequate sense of self may be at risk for developing any of the various personality disorders as defined by the *Diagnostic and Statistical Manual of Mental Disorders* (American Psychiatric Association, 2000).

From the Family Wellness perspective, individuals who have a realistic

FIGURE 1.1
DIFFERING PERSPECTIVES ON WHAT MAKES ME UNIQUELY ME

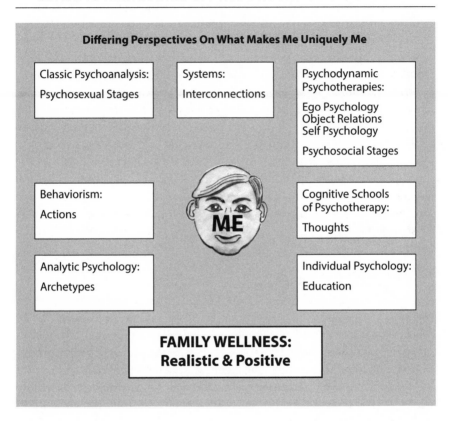

and positive sense of self are emotionally and psychologically healthy. An individual's sense of self develops from a combination of factors:

1. A genetically inherited and innate set of capabilities
2. Distinguishing physical characteristics that uniquely define the person as an individual
3. The environmental reality of birth date, birthplace, family of origin, and history
4. The definition of self developed from an individual's perception of self as reflected in the eyes of care providers from the earliest years of life

The Family Wellness model is not a separate school of psychotherapy. As such, the model accommodates just about any perspective on what it means to be Me. Family Wellness concepts can be adapted to, and incorporated into, many therapeutic orientations. The model supplements a clinician's understanding of how a person came to have a particular sense of self and provides practical skills for facilitating the amelioration of individual, couple, familial, or other interpersonal difficulties.

From the Family Wellness perspective, it is critical that individuals have a healthy, realistic, and positive sense of who they are. If they do, they are poised to take whatever action is necessary to meet their goals and to achieve satisfaction in life. Being an individual is one of the two critical jobs in finding balance in life. Knowing how to connect with others is the second, and equally important, component. That second factor is the subject of Chapter 2. Before we get to that topic, it is important to determine how practitioners use the Family Wellness model to assess an individual's sense of self.

THE ASSESSMENT OF INDIVIDUALITY

Assessment is defined by *Webster's* as "an appraisal, an evaluation." While this process sounds relatively simple, when dealing with human beings, assessment is an enormously complex task. Whether mental health professionals are assessing an individual, a couple, or a family system, a multitude of variables must be addressed. Some factors need immediate attention while others can be sorted out during the time when the therapist works with these individuals.

In this book, the Family Wellness model is used to help therapists in developing or enhancing skills for quick assessment. Some may argue that *quick* can be equated with *poor*. Naturally, slow assessment would be an ideal scenario, taking extensive time to look in depth at all of the cogent variables. In slow assessment, numerous formal assessment instruments could be used and the therapist would have the opportunity to evaluate people in their natural setting on at least several occasions. However, clinicians often must make almost split-second decisions about individuals. For example, in child abuse reporting cases, a decision as to whether to remove a child from a potentially lethal environment may be needed within moments. Other clinicians may work in emergency room settings where life-and-death decisions are being made. Some practitioners work in jails or other forensic settings where they have an extremely limited amount of time to directly assess an individual and must quickly form opinions and generate recommendations.

Some agencies and programs specialize in thorough, multidisciplinary assessment protocols. I do not wish to supplant those efforts. Such programs provide invaluable information to assess individuals, families, and situations. This book is intended to provide a perspective on how clinicians can quickly make assessments using the Family Wellness model with a reasonable degree of certainty about an individual and then initiate treatment planning that will inform practical interventions.

The Assessment Two-Step

As you begin the journey into quick assessment, I wish to remind you about two important early steps that will allow you to successfully complete your trip (Table 1.1). The first step is to make sure that you attend to your own personal safety, your client's safety, and the safety of others. The second step is to be aware of time considerations: Know how long the journey is and how quickly you must make your determinations about the person and the situation.

STEP ONE

The single most important assessment therapists must make has to do with safety, for both the mental health professional and the client. Is the person dangerous to himself or to others? If an individual is dangerous, the guiding principle is "safety first." Too often we hear of professionals who are injured or killed in the course of their work because either they did not attend to this issue or no adequate escape mechanism was in place. We know that some individuals are at the end of their rope and do not see alternatives beyond harming themselves or others. In such situations, the

TABLE 1.1
Two Early Steps for Assessment Success

Step One:	Safety First
	Personal Safety
	Client Safety
	Safety of Others
Step Two:	Time Considerations

professional, ethical, and moral imperative is to assist people by blowing on the embers of hope that may exist within them and by helping clients to develop safer alternative solutions.

The assessment of dangerousness is accomplished by utilizing all of our therapeutic skills through observing, listening, and intervening. Therapists observe the individual and situation, looking for signs of health as well as a sense of hopelessness. We observe the individual's mannerisms, statements, and physiological responses (sweating, pacing, breathing patterns). We listen to what the client is saying and to what he or she is not saying. We listen to whether the individual voices malicious intent toward self or others, to whether there are plans to effect the intent, and for signs of abject despair. People who are dangerous often have a foreshortened sense of the future due to severe depression, anxiety, or an absolute lack of hope. They believe that they have no alternatives.

Therapists intervene by contracting with individuals who have expressed or shown the potential for self-harm. We contract with them to call for help when they feel that they may harm themselves; we help them develop alternative strategies; and we make every effort to get clients to commit to a subsequent appointment or to some future additional action that they must take. If we assess that a clear and present danger exists for the individual or for others, then legal and ethical standards apply. Therapists must seek help for the client or potential victims so that all will be safe. Help may involve disclosure to others, contacting police or other authorities, and possibly involuntary confinement or commitment. To summarize, the first and most important assessment a therapist must make when engaging with individuals in a professional situation is to ascertain the level of safety and danger.

STEP TWO

After safety has been assessed, subsequent assessments depend upon the circumstances of our involvement with the person or situation. In the professional role, clinicians are usually responding to specific referral questions. In some cases therapists have a limited amount of time to make decisions about the individual's or family's condition, such as when we find ourselves in forensic environments (juvenile hall, jail, or hospital). Therapists may also have only a brief period of time to make decisions about interventions when we are in people's homes for crisis work, possibly involving situations such as domestic violence or child abuse. In other cases therapists have the luxury of time, such as when conducting full custody evaluations or in other formal assessment situations where we have a captive audience or the individual is motivated to provide as much information as possible to enable a positive assessment outcome. In these situations it is likely that formal testing and assessment instruments will be used. These instruments may have great value and add significantly to an understanding of individuals. However, because it is not always possible to obtain such formal assessments, the subject of this book is how the Family Wellness model can assist in making quick assessments that lead to practical interventions.

Salient factors that affect a sound assessment involve knowing a person's age, birth order, and family dynamics; developing a thorough family history; understanding the impact of culture and ethnicity on the individual; appreciating an individual's intellectual functioning level and its impact on educational attainment; knowing of any legal issues; attending to current life and familial situations; and knowing the person's strengths and future goals. To make the most accurate possible evaluation of the person, the therapist must consider and weigh all of the available data.

A major reason that accurate assessment can be difficult is because assessment is rooted in idiosyncratic theory. Theories abound about what makes people mentally and emotionally healthy or ill. Depending on which theory we espouse, our assessment will focus on specific aspects of that theory. In other words, our outcome is based on a set of variables that we determine to be salient issues to explore. To the degree that we focus on a specific set of variables, we may fail to recognize other factors that matter. It reminds me of the story of several blindfolded people touching various parts of an elephant and then describing the elephant in wildly different ways. Each person's description (assessment) was correct, yet each assessment was also wrong.

Effective treatment depends on accurate assessment. A mental health professional cannot possibly focus on all of the potential variables in each assessment, yet therapists must have a broad enough range of variables, based on theory, to ensure the best possible assessment given the limitations of science, time, and energy.

Assessment, at its heart, is the art of understanding a person, family, or situation at a given point in time. Good assessment can be conducted in a variety of ways. Some practitioners utilize a toolbox of assessment instruments. Some clinicians use test instruments that measure intelligence, personality, affective functioning, interpersonal skills, or sociopathy. Other practitioners rely on clinical judgment based on thorough interviews with a review of history, genogram, mental status examination questions, and extensive background information.

There is no single road that is the right or only way to accurately assess. The roads to assessment may be direct or winding, smooth or rough, level or inclined. Whatever the assessment path looks like, it must lead to the desired destination: obtaining an accurate picture of the individual, family, or situation.

The Assessment of Me

In this chapter, we use the Family Wellness model to determine the degree to which a person has a realistic and positive sense of self. Knowing that I have worth and value is foundational to my ability to speak up, to care about others enough to listen to them, and to want to solve problems together through cooperation. These are the key skills in the Family Wellness model. A healthy and well-balanced sense of Me is necessary to have a positive sense of We.

Regarding an individual's subjective assessment of Me, there are four possible options. Some people have no understanding of themselves as autonomous individuals. They know who they are only through their relationship with others. They do not see themselves as autonomous or individuated people who are able to function independently. A second group of people understand that they have a self, but they believe themselves to be without value or unworthy. They have a diminished or poor sense of self. They devalue themselves. A third group of individuals have a well-balanced appraisal of who they are. They know their strengths and weaknesses. They are able to function independently and also know how to relate to others in affirming, interdependent ways. They do not worry that they will be overwhelmed by others and lose themselves. They attack life directly and generally have a positive sense of well-being. Finally, some people believe themselves to be perfect in every dimension. They have an inflated sense of self that is not based on reality. They can only identify their strengths and they deny the presence of any weaknesses. Their assumptions about themselves may lead to a sense of entitlement when dealing with others. This stance can prevent cooperation and will inevitably cause interpersonal problems.

The first question in assessing an individual's sense of self is, "In which of these four quadrants does the individual fall?" The second question is, "How can a mental health professional quickly make that determination?"

The following four sections are intended to answer both questions by first outlining what it is like to be in each quadrant and then by providing some lines of inquiry that can illuminate whether an individual falls within that quadrant.

> 1. No sense of self
> 2. Poor sense of self
> 3. Good sense of self
> 4. Inflated sense of self

NO SENSE OF SELF

The state of having no sense of oneself as an autonomous individual is incredibly serious. It can lead to extreme angst and ultimate annihilation or it can lead to extreme dependence on others in order to define the self. In either event, the person's sense of self is absent.

> Susan came to my office for psychotherapy because her teenage daughter was acting out sexually and failing in school. Susan said that she "loved" the way I was able to provide her with useful information about parenting, how I was such a caring practitioner (in fact, "the best" therapist she had ever known!), and she appreciated the positive impact I was having on her family. Naturally, I thought Susan had good taste and was very astute.
>
> One day, Susan came to the office hoping to ask me a specific question about how to deal with her daughter's problems. The receptionist advised her that I was not available as I was at home, ill. Susan suddenly became agitated, enraged, and tearful. She started shouting at the receptionist in a very loud voice. As she stormed out of the office, she slammed the glass door behind her (nearly breaking it) as an exclamation point to display her frustration.
>
> At other times in our work together, Susan experienced suicidal ideation and showed tendencies toward actual suicide potentiality. She was unbelievably happy and content when she was connected with someone whom she admired, and she was extremely depressed and could become enraged when that person disappointed her (as always happened).

In essence, a person with no sense of self, like Susan, believes the following two sentences:

a. "I can only be me if I am connected to you."
b. "You can only be you if you are who I need you to be."

Susan exemplifies individuals who have severe difficulty with thinking of themselves as autonomous beings. Susan only feels good about herself when she is attached to others whom she considers to be perfect. In order to imbue others with such perfection, she has to overlook obvious imperfections. Susan feels revulsion and despair when reality supplants her idealization as she finds out that others are imperfect or unavailable. She has no independent sense of self and her life is a roller-coaster ride. Susan's dilemma is that since she perceives that she has no independent value, her only hope for a sense of personal worth is to connect with someone who is perfect. The other person's perfection provides her with what she believes that she lacks: value and worth. When the illusion of perfection is shattered by reality, Susan is confronted with her unbearable truth: that she is nobody and that she has no worth. The illusion of the other's perfection is untenable and the reality of Susan's perceived lack of worth is unbearable.

Susan may be diagnosed as having borderline personality disorder. Whatever the specific diagnostic label may be, we understand that a person like Susan needs to develop a sense of self. Without an appreciation of herself as a separate, autonomous individual, she will continue to be in despair when she is disappointed by others, and she will always be disappointed by others.

Assessing an individual with no sense of self requires that the therapist listen for evidence of how the person thinks about himself or herself. Open-ended questions directed at eliciting a person's sense of self are helpful, such as these:

1. Tell me three things you do well.

   Listen to how easily the person is able to state what he does well and how many items are identified. Many people have a hard time stating what they do well. However, most are able to do so if you wait and let them know that it is okay to "toot their own horn." Listen to how specifically the person is able to state what he does well. Vague statements likely demonstrate that he is not sure if he really has those skills.

2. Tell me what others would say about you.

   Listen for either a positive or negative slant on what the person says about what others would say about him. The responses will let you know how the client thinks about himself. People with no independent sense of self are often unable to determine what others would say about them, largely because they do not know what they would say about themselves. If they do identify some things others would say, the statements will likely be negative.

3. Tell me about your best personality traits.

Listen to whether individuals provide you with information about who they are versus what they do. People with no sense of self will often focus on what they do and can describe that in great detail. They think of themselves as human "doings" instead of human beings. Also listen to how often they describe themselves in relationship to others. They may only be able to describe who they are in connection with someone else. The others will likely be described as being larger than life. These clients will often believe themselves to be "less than" the others.

Look for extremes in the responses to these three lines of questioning. Many people may initially sound as if they fit this category. Upon further questioning, it may simply be that they have traits in the direction of having no sense of self. A determination that a person fits this category is a strong statement about the interpersonal problems that this client will likely experience without intervention from a mental health professional.

When working with individuals with no sense of self, clinicians need to be aware of the possibility of becoming placed on a pedestal and being idealized by these clients. Such a precarious placement will surely result in a difficult fall from grace because no one can ever satisfy another's expectation for perfection. Idealization is a tempting seducer and only brings ruin to both parties involved. Further, the interplay of transference and countertransference creates a shield that is difficult to penetrate with the sword of accurate assessment. We have to be careful to remain objective in the face of idealization. Therapists also need to be objective in the face of subsequent demonization. These are two sides of the same coin when we are working with an individual with no sense of self.

When a person does not believe that there is a unifying force that can be called self, he can easily become despondent and fearful. The individual may feel a sense of nothingness and experience severe existential angst. Such individuals, therefore, may present with severe depression and anxiety symptoms. They may also become desperate and begin to behave in extreme ways in their efforts to achieve equilibrium. They have no reference point that tells them who they are and what behavior is within their value system. Their desperation may cause them to behave in dangerous

ways as they seek to find a perfect friend, sexual partner, therapist, or any-
body who will help them in their travail. They may demand excessive
time and energy. They may be overly submissive or deferential to others,
even when it is not in their best interests. As such, they may be taken advantage of, used and abused, or rejected. Any of these outcomes will only
serve to confirm the lie that they already believe, which is that they have
absolutely no innate and independent value or worth.

POOR SENSE OF SELF
Some individuals definitely know that they are separate entities, selves
with certain characteristics. They just happen not to like who they are. If
people do not have an accurate and positive appraisal of their own self and
worth, they may come to loathe themselves. This self-deprecation may
exhibit itself in one of two ways. Some of these individuals are likely to
seek the approval of others and may be willing to do just about anything
to obtain that approval. They become very dependent and needy. Other
individuals with a poor sense of self will demand approval and will become
enraged when their need for approval is not satisfied. They become very
aggressive in their efforts to get their needs met. So, some individuals with
a poor sense of self become wimps and some become bullies.

> Frank is a police officer who knows how to control a situation on the streets.
> If he didn't, he could end up hurt or dead. He has honed professional skills
> in the assessment of people and situations. He has learned to use communi-
> cation skills, involving speaking up (with authority), listening (with dis-
> cernment), and finding solutions that work. He has received awards at work
> for using his people management skills and for diffusing difficult situations.
>
> After a hard day on the job, Frank goes home and looks forward to being
> greeted by his wife in an adoring, appreciative manner. Although he does
> not feel like talking much, he requires that his wife agree with him about
> everything, especially his opinions about politics. When she disagrees, he
> becomes sullen, develops a slow burn, and then gets sarcastic. He becomes
> verbally and, sometimes, physically abusive. He believes that his wife's dis-
> agreements reflect negatively on him as a man.
>
> Frank has excellent skills in the workplace, where he gets accolades from
> peers and management. His sense of self comes from what he does and,
> more importantly, from what his superiors tell him about what he does. At
> home, he desires similar appreciation. When he senses that he is not being
> acknowledged, he becomes aggressive in a desperate attempt to maintain a
> positive sense of self. At work, he finds his self-worth through his reflection
> in his management's eyes. At home, he can only see his self-worth through

the eyes of his wife. When she disagrees with him, he believes that she is denigrating him as a person in that she does not view him as intelligent. His grasp on self-worth is very tenuous.

Assessing whether an individual has a poor sense of self is important because of the implications for that person's emotional state and interpersonal functioning. A person with low self-esteem will likely not engage in healthy relationships with others, will seek others' approval, or will demand respect from others as an overreaction to internalized difficulties with self-respect.

Determining an individual's sense of self is generally accomplished by comparing that person's self-appraisal to his idea of how others think of him. Taking a person's family of origin history will usually reveal whether he believes that he was valued as an infant, a child, and an adolescent by his parents or care providers. The theory is that our sense of self develops at an early age from our perceptions of how our care providers view us. Questions about an individual's early childhood will usually reveal a great deal about his current sense of self. The following are some sample areas to explore regarding early experiences:

1. *What are the earliest things you remember from your childhood? What were you doing? What were others doing?*

   Often people who have had traumatic childhoods do not remember much about the early part of their life. Although some childhood amnesia is normal, extreme difficulty in remembering childhood events may suggest trauma. Therefore, be aware of the age of first memories. Traumatic events in childhood usually lead to lowered self-esteem. Young children are proud of their accomplishments. As children achieve mastery over certain developmentally guided behaviors, they develop an appropriate sense of pride. When parents and other care providers acknowledge a child's accomplishments, the child's self-worth increases. When others do not notice or diminish the child's achievements, the child's self-worth diminishes.

2. *What do you remember about your parents or others who cared for you? How did they treat you?*

   Children see the reflection of themselves in the eyes of those who care for them. That reflection is an important determinant of self-esteem. How parents or other care providers treat a child often results in confirmation to that child of whether she is valuable. If a person remembers parents who screamed, yelled, belittled, were perfectionistic, or otherwise showed the child that she did not measure up, then self-esteem was likely diminished. That same negative sense of self may continue into adulthood. If a person barely remembers her parents' presence, due to work or other commitments, and the parents rarely attended school or sports functions, her self-esteem very likely plummeted. The reverse, of course, is true. Close connections with affectionate parents generally increases self-esteem.

3. *What did you learn about yourself from the people that mattered most to you when you were a kid?*

First, listen to who the individual identifies as important players in her youth, including parents, grandparents, other relatives, neighbors, friends, teachers, coaches, pastors, and so on. Second, identify what she learned about herself. Was her value based on what she did or who she was? How did she measure up to the expectations of these important other individuals? The answers to these questions will clarify a great deal about the person you are assessing and how she developed her sense of self.

Remember that a sense of self is not necessarily simply related to whether or not an individual had a "good" or "happy" childhood. Neither is self-esteem always directly related to actual abilities or the lack thereof. There are often intervening variables that either reduce or increase a person's sense of self-worth, including life experiences, associations with significant others, a spiritual journey, health issues, and so on. Therefore, an exploration of an individual's history ought to be as broad as possible within the constraints of time.

Veronica worked in a skyscraper as a midlevel government bureaucrat. She was so beautiful that men and women from other floors in the building would find excuses to walk by her desk to catch a glimpse of her. She was stylish and carried herself with grace and aplomb. Women envied her and men yearned to be noticed by her so that they could catch the demure smile that she so gracefully showed. Veronica exuded sublime confidence.

Her therapist, however, knew a different Veronica. This Veronica was racked with self-doubt, lacked confidence, and saw herself as ugly. She knew that men paid attention to her but she could not understand why, other than thinking of them as being desperate if they sought her out and thought of her as desirable. She would often muse, "If they only knew the real me, they would run away." She had come to believe what important

They may buy minor things (soda, lunch) for others or may give larger, more expensive gifts. They are almost never willing to accept anything from others. Such clients need to know that they cannot buy approval. Such individuals also need to practice saying no. They need to know how to establish boundaries so that they can say yes to themselves.

Helping clients practice saying no to others and yes to themselves and to their own needs can be greatly beneficial. An individual with low self-esteem often does not know how to deal with others on an equal basis. He may put himself in a one-down position. He may acquiesce to others' needs and rarely consider his own.

In the therapy office, a client can be given several role-play scenarios wherein she is pushed by a peer to do something she does not want to do. The therapist can play the part of the peer. The task of the client is to practice speaking up, including the ability to say no. This exercise can support the development of a sense of the self as a valuable individual who is capable of independent action and choice. Sample topics for scenarios can include differences of opinion on where to go for a meal, where to go on vacation, or which movie to see. This role-playing in the office can be very beneficial in helping the client learn and practice the skill, which can then be generalized to real life. During the role-play, the client is coached to act in a new way. Positive steps in the desired direction are applauded and the client is redirected when she is having a hard time speaking up or negotiating.

When the client returns and recounts the experience of practicing this new skill with others, the therapist can reinforce successes and listen for reasons that the efforts at using the skill may not have produced the desired outcome. The therapist can make recommendations for change and assign that behavior as a homework task. The resulting practice will give the individual a better chance of obtaining what is desired. Always remember to applaud any effort in the desired direction.

DEMANDING AGREEMENT

If an individual demands acquiescence and agreement from others, encouragement to learn how to handle disagreement will be a predominant intervention. A person who demands that others agree with him and feels devastated or enraged when they do not is usually feeling weak and inferior. The strong facade is often a cover for feelings of inadequacy.

An excellent initial exercise to help develop awareness is to have the individual stand on one foot while pointing out to him how out of balance one feels when standing on just one foot. As the person starts to lose balance, ask what he can do to stabilize himself. Possible answers include holding onto something in the room, such as a chair, sofa, or desk. Another possibility is to hold onto someone else. The final, and best, answer is to put the other foot down. Individuals who get out of balance sometimes try to find equilibrium by becoming involved with something or someone. This process, while apparently temporarily solving the problem, tends to create larger problems in the future.

The concept behind the one-foot exercise is that the best outcome results when a person can find balance within himself. People who connect with others when they have only one foot planted on the ground run the risk of becoming involved in a codependent relationship. This codependency occurs because unhealthy people tend to connect with other unhealthy people. Each person needs the other person to be there for him in order to continue feeling whole or balanced. When individuals plant the other foot on the ground, they have a much better chance of connecting with others in a healthy manner. Healthy people tend to connect with other healthy people.

Healthy people know that when someone disagrees with them the difference of opinion does not negate their worth as individuals. People who do not have a good sense of self, however, may feel attacked when someone disagrees with them. One way to demonstrate that it is possible for people to disagree and yet have the ability to stay connected involves a garbage can.

Instruct a couple to simulate an argument or disagreement while facing one another. If only one client is present, the therapist can play the part of the person's spouse or friend. Place a garbage can between the two people, which forces them to move apart. This demonstrates the separation that automatically occurs when they argue. Next, put the garbage can in front of the couple and ask them to sit closer together, while they both face the can. This placement allows both of them to look at the garbage can while they argue. This activity demonstrates that couples can disagree and still be able to stay or get close to each other. Despite their disagreement, this couple can focus on solving problems together. This intervention suggests that disagreement does not have to equal denigration or separation. In fact, the development of a better sense of self can provide the foundation that actually allows people to disagree yet get closer to one another. Solving problems together develops intimacy.

Good Sense of Self

Individuals who feel good about themselves do not generally seek treatment. They have an adequate friendship network and support system because they use their speaking, listening, and cooperating skills to manage their lives, any stress, and the issues that arise through the process of living.

If individuals with a good sense of self come for treatment, it is important to let them know which skills they are already using well. This affirmation reinforces the importance of continued use of these skills for maintaining an emotionally healthy and balanced life.

Sometimes, individuals want something better for themselves or for someone important in their life. Interventions with relatively healthy individuals will likely focus on specific goals. Sometimes, the person will need help in focusing on exactly what they want. The Family Wellness model uses a three-part outline for helping people to achieve their goals: know what you want, say what you want, and get what you want.

Knowing what we want is often a difficult task, even for healthy people. When people are asked what they want, they often begin by saying what they do not want. For example, "I don't want people to walk all over me." The therapist can help clients focus on what they do want. For example, "You want others to listen to your needs. Give me an example of something you want your friends to know that you need."

Sometimes an individual will identify several goals. In these situations, the therapist can ask the person to focus on only one goal, with a comment such as, "Say one thing that you would like." If he states several goals, the therapist can say, "Pick one."

Often a person will state the goal in very general terms, such as, "I want to be happier." The therapist can help the client to get more specific. For example, "What will it look like when you are happier? What will you be doing? What will others around you be doing?" This "funneling" process is one of helping the person focus, moving from the negative to the positive, and then from the general to the specific. When we make the goals SMART, their achievement becomes much more likely. Getting people to be specific by making goals that are measurable, attainable, reasonable, and time limited is a very practical intervention that leads to success.

Healthy, well-balanced individuals with a good sense of self already have most of the resources that they need to achieve their goals. Treatment with these clients will likely be short term. Interventions will primarily focus on helping them to achieve their identified goals.

Inflated Sense of Self

Treatment interventions with people who think too highly of themselves will often be very difficult. Such people may not see the need to alter any aspects of themselves. Instead, they will likely think everyone else needs to change. The person who needs to change, in the client's mind, may be the spouse, the children, the coworker, the boss, or whoever is involved as the reason that he was referred for treatment. His self-assessment is that he is just fine.

Although intervention with these individuals can start with reiterating their strengths, as a means of connecting with them, the therapist must quickly help them focus on areas that do need change. This is not an easy task. The client will likely say, "If my spouse would simply change, we would both be much happier." The therapist needs to help the client refocus on what he or she can do to create a better chance that the spouse will change. In other words, the therapist reminds the client that no one can change another person. We can only change ourselves. As some problem has resulted in referral to a therapist, a good question for the client is, "What can you change that will give you both a better chance of being happy?" The therapist must help the individual take personal responsibility for effecting change in any relationship.

Treatment interventions need to focus on the balance between recognizing clients' strengths and appreciating that they also have deficits. Helping a client to focus on effecting personal change provides the best opportunity for others to change. The marketing concept of "what's in it for me" may be a useful intervention tool with this type of client. Let him know that if he changes, his partner has a greater chance of changing, probably resulting in a more harmonious relationship.

To demonstrate the importance of changing ourselves to change a relationship, have couples complete the following exercise. Have each person write on a piece of paper what he or she wants to gain from this session, course of treatment, or retreat. Then ask each person to write on another piece of paper what they want their spouse to learn. This second list will likely be longer than the first. Instruct them to tear up the second list. Explain, "This treatment will work best if each person focuses on himself or herself. This treatment is for you, in order to help you have a better chance of getting what you want. When we change, there is a better chance that the people around us will change."

SUMMARY

The psychotherapeutic endeavor involves making sound assessments of individuals for the purpose of developing treatment plans that establish the goals of treatment and specify practical interventions that will help effect change.

Interventions for change work best when the therapist adopts a therapeutic stance with the people being served. That therapeutic stance can be conceptualized through the acronym CAGE: concern, acceptance, genuineness, and empathy (adapted from Yalom & Leszcz, 2005).

Concern refers to the fact that we care about the people we treat. We have their best interests at heart. If you do not care for your clients, please do something else. Get another job. Acceptance means that we are nonjudgmental. We attempt to understand clients as best we can and we appreciate their innate value and worth. Genuineness means that we are real. We do not put on a facade. We actually are who we say we are. Empathy is the ability to know our clients through the prism of their own perspective. We try to understand what it is like for them to be who they are—to walk in their shoes.

The therapist who takes on this therapeutic stance is in the best position to join with clients on the journey to which they have invited us. This cooperative venture is the essence of the psychotherapeutic experience. The connection forged between therapist and client engenders trust and hope. When clients have trust in the therapist and hope for the future, they are more likely to take the leap of faith from the known to the unknown. It takes faith and guts for clients to attempt to achieve their goals through the interventions that we have codeveloped with them.

The self is a complex and multifaceted entity that is understood and described by philosophers and mental health professionals in many ways. From the Family Wellness perspective, individuals have to complete two tasks to be emotionally healthy. The first job is having a realistic and positive sense of self: knowing who they are and appreciating their own worth and value as people. After they figure out what it is to be Me, the second major job of being a healthy individual is knowing how to connect with others: learning how to be We.

2

Connect With Others

The Importance of Being We

THE HUMAN BEING can be understood only in context. Despite numerous important aspects of being human, the most important determinant of a person's sense of self is his connection, or lack of connection, with others. Irvin D. Yalom, an existential and interpersonal psychiatrist, said, "We are at all times obligated to consider the human being in the matrix of his or her interpersonal relationships" (Yalom & Leszcz, 2005, p. 19).

The modern schools of dynamic psychotherapy are based on the importance of interpersonal relationships. Their theorists include Karen Horney, Erich Fromm, and Harry Stack Sullivan. In particular, Sullivan's interpersonal theory of psychiatry posits that an individual's personality results almost entirely from interaction with other significant human beings (Sullivan, 1953).

The Family Wellness model proposes that individuals have two jobs: be an individual and connect with others. Emotionally healthy individuals tend to connect with other healthy individuals. Likewise, people with huge needs tend to connect with other people with huge needs, thus establishing codependent, unhealthy relationships.

At the heart of an individual's sense of feeling connected with others (or not) is the theoretical concept of attachment. Social attachment is of primary importance in the life of an infant. Without adequate attachment, the baby is at risk of actual physical annihilation without someone to assume the dual roles of provider and protector. The newborn requires someone who provides both food and shelter, thus ensuring survival. Social attachment is defined as "the process through which people develop specific, positive emotional bonds with others" (Newman & Newman, 1999, p. 150).

At birth there is no particular attachment to any adult. Any adult who provides for the baby's needs will do. However, before the end of the infant's first year of life, the baby has developed a very strong emotional preference for specific care providers.

John Bowlby (1988) posited that the attachment behavior system is an organized pattern of signals from infants and the adult responses to those signals that results in a protective, trusting relationship. Bowlby's focus was on explaining the process whereby an infant ensures that a care provider will attend to the infant's needs, thus ensuring survival. The nurturing response of adults to infant signals is seen as a complementary behavior system that we call parenting or caregiving (Bowlby, 1988; Ainsworth, 1985).

The ability of infants and care providers to work together in dyadic relationships for the safety and survival of infants is seen as a survival skill in infants and toddlers. The synchrony of such interactions (Isabella & Belsky, 1991) bodes well for attachment, a sense of security, safety, comfort, affective engagement, and preference for specific care providers above all others. The quality and quantity of synchronized interactions impact the infant's confidence in the caregiver's capacity to provide for the infant's safety (Cox, Owen, Henderson, & Margand, 1992).

Ainsworth (1973, 1985) describes five stages in the development of attachment in infants (Table 2.1). In the first stage, infants engage in a variety of behaviors that serve to maintain closeness with a care provider or to bring the care provider to the infant. These behaviors, including crying, cooing, smiling, gazing, grasping, and so on, evoke the desire to nurture,

TABLE 2.1
Five Stages of Attachment

	Task	Age
1.	Connection/survival	First 3 months
2.	Preferential responsiveness	3–6 months
3.	Physical proximity	6–9 months
4.	Internal representation	9–12 months
5.	Increased behaviors/connection	1 year and beyond

or care for, the infant. The behaviors apparently are not aimed at a par-ticular or specific person. Through these behaviors, the infant learns a great deal about the responsiveness of care providers. This stage occurs in the first 3 months of life.

The second stage, from about ages 3 months to 6 months, involves an infant's preferential responsiveness to a few familiar individuals rather than to strangers. Infants during this stage tend to be more demonstratively excited when certain people arrive and to be upset when these people leave. The person who is "chosen" to be the infant's caregiver is likely to be even more responsive to the infant, which then makes the infant even more responsive to that individual. In other words, attachment is deep-ened and accelerated partly due to a behavior-response spiral.

The third stage of attachment occurs from about ages 6 to 9 months. During this period, infants generally seek physical proximity to the ob-jects of their attachment. Babies become more capable of moving them-selves to be close to people or things to which they desire connection.

The fourth stage of attachment is from about 9 to 12 months. It is pos-tulated that during this time babies form their first internal representation of their caregivers. In this attachment scheme, the specific characteristics of the care provider, including the infant's expectations of the caregiver's responses to the infant's behaviors, are put together in a complex mental representation of the anticipated responses of a care provider. This repre-sentation allows the infant to appreciate a sense of self as valuable or not, as well as to know to what degree the environment is safe to explore and what the limits of that exploration may be.

The fifth stage of attachment, which comes at about 1 year and beyond, is when children use an increased range of behaviors to influence their parents to meet their needs for closeness and connection. During this stage, children may ask parents to come near them, to hold them, to play with them, and to take them places. These behaviors become strategies that young children use to modify their parents' behavior as well as to satisfy their needs for connection and safety. New strategies may be de-veloped by children during times of extreme stress and perceived periods of potential danger or anticipated abandonment or rejection.

An individual's sense of attachment and a family's capacity for attach-ment varies from individual to individual, from one parent-child dyad to another, and from family to family. Infants and children require adults who are able to respond well to the infants' signals and who are capable of

TABLE 2.2
Four Patterns of Attachment

1. Secure
2. Anxious-avoidant
3. Anxious-resistant
4. Disorganized

providing for each child's needs for safety, reassurance, comfort, and connection (Tracy & Ainsworth, 1981).

Beside the five stages of attachment, four patterns of attachment have been identified (Table 2.2): secure, anxious-avoidant, anxious-resistant, and disorganized (Ainsworth, Blehar, Waters, & Wall, 1978; Bretherton, 1990).

Infants who have a secure attachment explore their environment and interact with strangers while the mother is present. When the mother returns after an absence, such infants greet her and want interaction. The mother's return signals safety and exploration of the environment continues. These infants cry less than other babies (Tracy & Ainsworth, 1981; Ainsworth, 1985). They are more cooperative with their mothers' requests. These infants expect their care providers to be accessible and responsive based on having behaved that way in the past when infants prompted for connection.

Infants who have an anxious-avoidant attachment avoid interaction with their mothers after separation and avoid parental efforts at interaction. They show less distress while they are alone than other infants. Mothers of infants in this category seem to be rejecting of their babies. They do not hold or play with their babies as much as other parents. These infants cry more often and are not easily soothed. Despite their apparent lack of desire for contact, these infants are very distressed when separated from their parents.

Infants who have an anxious-resistant attachment are extremely cautious in the presence of strangers. They dramatically decrease exploration behaviors when the mother is not available. When the mother returns, these infants are angry at the parent and are hard to soothe. Mothers of children in this category appear to be more inconsistent in their responsiveness to infant signals for attention and connection. At times, these parents ignore the infant's cries of distress. At other times they respond in inappropriate ways to the infant's needs. Therefore, these infants appear to have an internal representation of care providers who are highly unpredictable.

Infants who have a disorganized attachment do not appear to have a coherent strategy for managing the stress of the absent parent. These infants behave in unpredictable ways that seem to convey extreme fear or confusion (Belsky, Campbell, Cohn, & Moore, 1996). Mothers of these infants appear to have serious deficits in maternal behaviors and may have a variety of psychological problems. These parents may be abusive or depressed, or may exhibit other forms of mental illness. These parents may be psychologically unavailable and unpredictable (van Ijzendoorn, Goldberg, Kroonenberg, & Frenkel, 1992).

Research shows the importance of secure attachments for infants later in life. For example, secure attachment in infancy is associated with positive capacities when the child is 3 to 5 years old. Securely attached infants grow into children who have greater resilience, self-control, and curiosity (Vaughn, Egeland, Stroufe, & Waters, 1979). On the other hand, infants with a disorganized attachment pattern grow into children who are very hostile and aggressive. Problems with infant attachment have been linked to becoming withdrawn, socially hypervigilant, and resistant to comfort. Problems with infant attachment have also been linked to inadequate discriminatory abilities, being overly friendly, and attaching to any new person (DeAngelis, 1997).

In summary, infant attachments appear to be partly dependent on the nascent personality and partly due to the responsiveness of the parents or care providers. This interplay between who we are and who the important others in our lives are forms the foundation for our history, the growth of our personality, the strength of our sense of self, and the root of our ability to connect with others. In other words, we are the product of our history. The good news is that we do not have to be prisoners of that history.

ASSESSMENT: CAN I BE WE WITHOUT LOSING ME?

We know that the strength of the attachment that an infant forms with care providers greatly influences the formation of later relationships (Ainsworth, 1989). Children with secure attachments are likely to enjoy close friendships in their preschool years (Park & Waters, 1989). Children who

FIGURE 2.1
CONTINUA FOR CONNECTION: X- AND Y-AXES

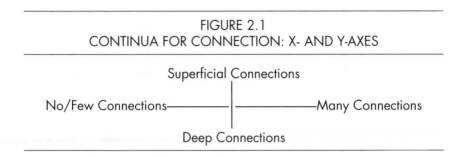

Superficial Connections

No/Few Connections——————|——————Many Connections

Deep Connections

have secure parental attachments are more likely to attribute positive intentions to peers while children with anxious attachments are more likely to be distrustful of peers.

As people move from childhood through adolescence to adulthood, the attachments and internal representations that were forged in the very earliest years of life significantly influence expectations within adult relationships. Adult relationships can be evaluated using the Family Wellness model in three specific arenas: the capacity for friendship, the willingness to engage in romantic intimacy, and parenting skills.

Assessment in each of the first two arenas (friendship and romantic intimacy) results in the placement of individuals on two intersecting continua of number of connections with others on the x-axis and depth of connections on the y-axis (Figure 2.1). Assessment in the third arena (parenting) is based on an individual's capacity to be both a leader and a model.

Assessment outcomes will identify individuals as being in one of four quadrants: (1) few and superficial connections, (2) few yet deep connections, (3) many superficial connections, and (4) many deep connections (Figure 2.2). Placement on this grid in each of these first two arenas will suggest treatment plans and practical interventions using the Family Wellness model.

FIGURE 2.2
FOUR QUADRANTS FOR CONNECTION

Few and Superficial Connections	Many Superficial Connections
Few yet Deep Connections	Many Deep Connections

Capacity for Friendship

Friendship is an intimate connection with another. To develop friendship, individuals need to feel good about themselves and to have a realistic and positive sense of self. The willingness to invest in friendship presupposes the knowledge that one has something of value to offer others while concomitantly seeking connection with someone who is valued. Friendship develops as a person is increasingly able to trust someone else. A friendship can only be as healthy as the individual members of that relationship. When individuals do not feel good about themselves, they are likely to either isolate themselves or forge relationships that are unhealthy and unbalanced.

Trust refers to an appraisal of the predictability, dependability, and genuineness of another person (Rempel, Holmes, & Zanna, 1985). Risk is the willingness to put ourselves in a position of vulnerability with respect to others. Our capacity to trust and risk are developed in the earliest periods of life and are based on our relationships with our care providers.

As infants and toddlers, if we cry and someone shows up to find out what is wrong and attempts to help us in our distress, we begin to believe that we are valuable and that we can trust this specific person to look out for our needs. If we cry and the care provider does not attend to us or yells, "Shut up!" then we question both our worth and the ability of that person to show up and be available to care for our needs.

Later in life, our interpersonal experiences either support or challenge our earliest assumptions about ourselves, our capacity to trust others, and our safety in relationship with others.

Although people differ in their need and desire for friendship based on personality, every individual needs at least some deep, significant friendships. Without friendship, people can feel alone and adrift without an anchor. With friendship to buoy us, whatever problems we encounter can be dealt with directly. We can count on support and encouragement from friends through our hard times. We can also count on them to tell us when we are making mistakes because they care about us and do not want us to face the potential negative consequences of our poor choices. Friends can sometimes save us from ourselves. Friendship can be very good medicine.

In assessing an individual's relative well-being, therapists look at the nature of the friendships that the person has been able to form. This assessment can provide us with valuable information about a person's past experiences as well as her potential capacity for forming new and healthier friendships. Friendship can also provide a forum for practicing pro-social skills.

> Sofia told me in our initial session that she did not have any friends. The only adults she spoke with were members of her extended family. Even interacting with them was difficult. She had learned not to trust others when she was young. She knew that others would "talk about you and abandon you for any reason." Sofia had never really had anyone whom she would describe as a best friend. Although she was okay with not having friends, she acknowledged that she sometimes felt lonely.

In assessing the capacity for friendship, therapists are not looking simply at how many friends a person has. Having many friendships is not necessarily better than having few friends. It is not the number but the quality of friendship that matters. What matters is an individual's capacity to develop deep connections versus only superficial connections. The fact that Sofia never experienced any satisfying friendships reveals much about the learned lack of trust from her past and difficulties with risk in the present. Without intervention, this combination bodes poorly for Sofia's capacity to enjoy satisfying friendships in her future.

Assessment questions related to the quantity and quality of friendships are very important. We assess children by asking them to name a few of their friends. Avoid asking questions that can be answered with simple "yes" or "no" responses. Make open-ended statements or enquiries such as, "Tell me the names of a few of your friends" or "Tell me about your best friends."

If an individual cannot name any friends, this response is obviously a red flag. It may mean that the person has not developed a secure attachment and that his asocial lifestyle may be cementing into an isolative lifelong experience. Such a lifestyle is extremely difficult, especially for children. Children have the very important psychosocial task of developing friendships. If they fail to manage this task well, they may be ostracized by other children, may be bullied, may have very poor self-esteem, and are at risk for the development of mental and emotional problems.

When a child is able to provide a few names of friends, the therapist can ask follow-up questions such as, "Tell me three things you like about that person. What are some things you do together? Who gets to pick what you do together?" These questions often elicit information useful in determining the nature of children's peer associations, especially about the power differentials in their various friendships. The therapist can then begin to determine if there are specific patterns of interaction between the child and friends.

With adults, therapists normally ask questions about their past, such as, "Tell me about your longest friendship. How did you get together? What has maintained your friendship over all these years? What do you do to stay connected?"

Some adults live most of their lives in one place. These adults likely have long-term friendships. If they do not, the therapist would explore what has occurred in their lives to break the friendships. Others have moved frequently. Some adults who move frequently manage to maintain friendships and learn how to quickly develop new friendships. Other adults lose old friendships and connect with new ones easily. Yet others lose the old friendships and fail to develop new friends. Each of these behavioral patterns of developing, breaking, and redeveloping friendship can provide useful information about the nature of an individual's friendships as well as about the capacity to develop new friendships.

The saying goes, "In order to make friends, you have to be friendly." If the therapist assumes that part of an individual's mental and emotional well-being involves the capacity to form friendships, it makes sense that we can count the number of friends an individual has and have some notion of how healthy the individual is. Unfortunately, it would be a mistake to assume that all friendships are created equal. The sheer number of friendships does not guarantee emotional well-being, except for one number: zero. A person's ability to trust others and to take risks is a great determinant of the potential quality of the friendships in which the individual engages. The clinician, therefore, needs to look at the depth of friendship relationships.

In assessing a person's capacity for friendship, the Family Wellness model specifically looks at both the quality and the quantity of the individual's friendship relationships. It is assumed that deeper relationships are healthier than superficial relationships. However, more friendships are not necessarily better than fewer friendships, unless the person has no friendships.

Willingness to Engage in Romantic Intimacy

Adult intimate romantic relationships may be assessed along the same dimensions as infant attachments, including such factors as the desire to maintain physical contact with the loved one, an expectation of mutuality in giving and receiving disclosures from one's partner, the importance of providing and receiving comfort and reassurance, the increase and decrease of anxiety and distress based on the presence or absence of one's partner, and the exclusive or preferential nature of certain relationships.

People fall in love throughout the life span. Falling in love based on need (e.g., the need for comfort, companionship, sex, or economic security) is normal and is not a problem. Falling in love based on huge need (being inconsolable when alone, feeling abjectly isolated, being unable to cope without a sexual outlet, not having the capacity to survive financially without another) is a huge problem.

Falling in love based on huge need is like standing on one foot and beginning to wobble. We may reach out for anything or anyone to help stabilize us. When we demonstrate this concept in the therapist's office or in a classroom, the something we reach for may be a desk or a chair. The someone may be the person next to us or the therapist. In real life, the anything we reach for may be alcohol, drugs, indiscriminate sexuality, or work. The anyone may be whoever is conveniently available despite misgivings we may have about them (e.g., they are already married, are chronically unemployed, are incapable of commitment, have substance abuse problems, or are immature).

If we reach out for someone else to help us feel more stable, we may make big errors in judgment precisely because of our personal instability. It is like being pushed to make a decision before we have gathered all of the best available information. Further, the person who might find us attractive in our instability may also have a complementary huge need to meet our need. That dynamic between two individuals often yields a codependent relationship.

> Sam and Judy have been married for over 20 years. He is handsome and she is beautiful. He is successful at work and she cares for the home and focuses on raising their children. They do volunteer work together in their church's youth program. To everyone they seem to be the perfect couple. Unfortunately, they find themselves in the therapist's office because they are on the brink of divorce, even though they do not believe in divorce as an option for them.
>
> Sam has had a significant problem with pornography for years. He also engaged in at least two extramarital affairs that Judy knows about. Recently, Sam almost got fired because he was watching Internet pornography on his computer at work. Judy is afraid that she and her children cannot survive without her husband's income. She has begrudgingly forgiven Sam for his

peccadilloes and has repeatedly suppressed her desire to file for divorce. Judy still believes that their marriage was "made in heaven" and that Sam is the love of her life. "He completes me!" Sam and Judy cannot live with each other and they cannot live without each other.

In assessing adults' capacity for connection, mental health professionals generally take a detailed personal and familial history. They often use a genogram to have a pictorial representation of the individual in context. Therapists identify the nature of current and past relationships, especially romantic connections that are significant because of the length of connection or depth of affection. Therapists also consider brief romantic relationships, including the frequency, nature, and relative intensity of these relationships. The Family Wellness model proposes that assessing an individual's capacity for connecting in romantic intimacy involves developing information about the quantity and quality of those romantic connections.

Most people have romantic and sexual histories that follow what is considered normal relative to the *social clock*, the time frame within which certain behaviors are expected and are developmentally appropriate based on what usually happens within the general population of a given cohort or group of people. Roughly speaking, these relationships often begin in late adolescence and young adulthood.

Some individuals have very early sexual experiences due to incest, molestation, or rape. Others have engaged in early sexual experimentation or play. These experiences may have been voluntary and consensual, coerced by force or threat of force, or engaged in for the allure of some benefit to the young person. These early experiences may have been with approximately same-age partners or with older people. Such experiences can be traumatic. Individuals may seek out these experiences for personal gain or due to curiosity. All of these early sexual situations must be thoroughly reviewed based on the individual's statements of their impact as well as being evaluated through corroborating evidence (e.g., impact on grades, family life, sexual inhibition or promiscuity, criminality, or level of affective responsiveness).

Others have an absolute dearth of romantic or sexual history. The absence of such relationships is not the primary diagnostic issue. The main issue is the impact of the lack of romantic or sexual intimacy on the individual. What is important to consider is the impact in every area of personality and behavior: how the individual thinks about himself or herself, what is felt, and how the person functions. The dual questions to consider are these: Is the person functioning well in the areas of love, work, and play despite the lack of intimate connection with others? Is the person depressed or anxious because of the romantic history and life circumstances?

Still other people have a bountiful history of intimate relationships. These intimate encounters may be short term and frequent or infrequent; long term and frequent or infrequent; they may coincide or co-occur with other intimate encounters; they may be serial; or they may have no discernible pattern. Again, the primary assessment issue is not the number and frequency of intimate relationships; it is the impact on the individual's life, quality of functioning, and well-being.

It is also important for the therapist to consider the impact of sexual or romantic behaviors on the individual's partners. That information may be more difficult to obtain because it is usually difficult to have access to any partners. However, questions regarding individuals' sense of the impact of their behavior on their partners may yield valuable information. The mental health practitioner will need to use clinical judgment to determine the relative merit of an individual's own assessment of the impact of his or her behavior on others. The nature of the individual's response to the question of impact can tell the therapist a great deal about the individual's capacity for empathy and acceptance of responsibility. It can also tell the clinician much about how an individual assesses the worth and value of another individual as compared to his or her own worth.

Parenting Skills

In assessing the capacity for connection, parenting ability can be understood, in part, as being based on an individual's attachment to his or her parents during the formative years. Adults who had a secure attachment in their own infancy are more likely to be able to comfort and respond to their children's needs. Adults whose attachments were unpredictable or even hostile are more likely to have problems coping with their own infants' needs (Ricks, 1985, in Newman & Newman, 1999).

An adequate assessment of parenting skills requires that the therapist know what *good enough* parenting is. There are a variety of ways of addressing the issue of what constitutes good parenting, including academic and practical books on the subject and many excellent parent education programs. The Family Wellness model, which has existed since 1980 and is utilized by numerous individuals, families, and agencies throughout the world, is one such program.

The concepts in the Family Wellness model are simple and easy to understand. This parenting model is based on the concept that healthy parents are both *leaders* and *models*. As leaders, parents make rules, stick together, and stay in charge. As models, parents make time for their children, encourage their children, listen to their children, and talk together with their children. Parents are usually good at one of these two tasks and not as good at the other: They either know how to be in charge or they know how to play. What children need is for each parent to be good at both jobs. To the degree that each parent is able to both lead and model in a balanced way, the children do better. Assessment of good enough parenting, therefore, is based on an individual's capacity to be both a leader and a model.

The Family Wellness model also posits that parents are good enough to the degree that they can utilize three skills to be leaders and models: Healthy parents know how to *speak, listen,* and *cooperate.*

Speaking up is based on the idea that each person has innate worth and value simply because of being human. To speak up demonstrates the ability to be a good leader. To speak up requires a degree of self-confidence or self-esteem. It presumes the capacity to individuate. Healthy people, when they are speaking up, start most sentences with the word "I": for example, "I feel, I think, I need, I want, I would like, or I would appreciate." Speaking up is about connecting with others from an above position: from a position of authority and responsibility.

Listening is based on the concept that others have innate worth and have something of value to say. To listen demonstrates the ability to be a good follower. To listen requires the capacity to consider others as being important. Listening also demonstrates the capacity to value input from others. It is the ability to connect with others and to care about them. Healthy individuals listen to words, feelings, and energy level. When these people are listening, they start most sentences with the word "You": for example, "You're tired, you're angry, you're frustrated, or you're sad." Listening is about connecting with others from a below position: from a position of deference and respect.

Cooperation demonstrates the capacity for seeking solutions that are, as much as possible, acceptable to everyone involved. We want a "good deal" for ourselves and for others as well. Cooperation is the attitude and negotiation is the ability to find solutions that work. Healthy people generally cooperate when they seek a win-win and use the word "We." For

FIGURE 2.3
CONNECTION WITH OTHERS: POWER DIFFERENTIAL

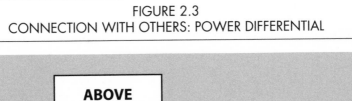

example, "We can, we will, we must, or we need." Cooperation is about connecting with others from a beside (coequal) position (Figure 2.3).

Assessing the strengths and weaknesses of an individual's capacity for parenting will assist the therapist in determining the individual's relative capacity for connecting with others. Therefore, the mental health professional needs to determine whether a parent is capable of making rules, working cooperatively, and staying in charge of the family. The clinician also needs to assess to what degree the parent makes time for children, encourages them, listens, and talks together with them. These capabilities are best assessed via questions about how parents handle difficult situations as well as through observation of clients' actual family dynamics. Much can be learned through observation. Therapists, however, must remember the social science truism that observation of a thing changes the thing. Whenever possible, therapists should learn about an individual's ability to manage the family through questioning all individuals within the family.

To the degree that an individual knows and practices good parenting skills, that person is likely to know how to connect with others. A parenting skills assessment is deemed useful information in helping the practitioner know how to intervene with a particular family that may be in crisis. Through such an assessment, the clinician can determine whether the individual requires additional help in being a leader or a model. The therapist can also assess whether the individual needs to speak, listen, or co-operate to a greater or lesser degree.

Even when individuals are not exhibiting good parenting skills, it is likely that they are capable of learning these skills. This is a basic premise of the Family Wellness model: Skills can be taught and learned. When parents fail to protect children or overtly abuse children, questions arise about how long it will take for parents to become better at their job of being parents and under what circumstances that should occur. The primary issue in difficult family situations, such as those faced by mental health professionals who work in children's protective services, is the question of children's safety. Clearly, safety is of primary importance in making these difficult choices.

Sound assessment of an individual's capacity for friendship, the willingness to engage in romantic intimacy, and parenting abilities leads to the development of treatment plans and practical interventions. All of these decisions and actions affect the adults involved and dramatically impact children's lives. In these situations extraordinary care needs to be taken to ensure an accurate assessment, safety for children, and dignity for all.

TREATMENT PLANNING: ON FINDING BALANCE BETWEEN ME AND WE

Having assessed an individual in terms of number and depth of connections with others in the arenas of friendship and intimate romantic relationships, and along the dimensions of being leaders and models for parenting abilities, the mental health professional is ready to develop a treatment plan.

People often seek services due to problems with connection. The presenting problem may be a sense of isolation (the lack of social support) as a perennial problem or due to recent or impending broken relationships (either in friendship, romance, or the family). The presenting problem, at the other extreme, may be about a loss of self due to excessive connection, which therapists call *enmeshment*. These people lose their autonomy and sense of self because they subsume their needs to the needs of others. They may not even recognize that they have individual needs.

Any treatment plan must take into account the reason(s) for referral, which include the presenting problems or issues, the individual's perspective on his situation, his strengths and weaknesses, and the resources currently or potentially available.

On the continua of number and depth of connections, there is no "right" location on each continuum that is considered optimally healthy. Nevertheless, therapists generally think of the extremes as unhealthy positions and use terms such as isolation or enmeshment to describe them. Every other spot on the continuum is viewed as potentially healthy depending on the individual's personality and socialization needs. Having friendships and romantic relationships and the relative depth of these connections are partly based on an individual's history, current skills and abilities, and the opportunities available at any point in time. Good assessment on the dual continua will point practitioners in the direction of what individuals need and want as well as the resources that they need in order to achieve their goals, which is the essence of a useful treatment plan.

People often need treatment services because they are unhappy with their position on a continuum and desire to be at a different spot. They frequently do not know how to identify where they are or where they want to be. A good treatment plan will help clients identify where they are, point them to where they want to be, and identify the resources that they need to achieve their goals.

Capacity for Friendship

Mitchell wrote that individuals can only be understood within a tapestry of past and present relationships (Mitchell, 1988). To be a human being is to have significant interconnections with others. To truly know a human being is to understand the interconnections.

Friend relationships are crucial for children. Although children begin life having no friends, they begin to form preferential relationships over time. First, infants identify care providers who will attend to their needs and ensure their survival. Next, children develop the capacity to play, which they generally practice with parents and other available individuals such as older siblings and others in child care settings. Research shows that during the toddler years (ages 2 and 3), the more time toddlers have to play with others, the more complex their fantasy play will be (Eckerman & Didow, 1996).

As children grow into early school age (4 to 6 years) they continue developing their sense of self and base self-esteem predominantly on their increasingly large circle of relationships outside of their family. Their self-esteem is greatly influenced by their perceptions of how others evaluate them. Children modify their self-evaluation based on messages of love, support, and approval that they receive from others, from their specific attributes and competencies, and from an assessment of these aspects of self in comparison with others and based on their ideal self (Pelham & Swann, 1989).

Through these findings, we see the importance of messages received about being loved, admired, and seen as successful. Failure in these areas can lead to feelings of worthlessness. Even very young children can make global negative statements about themselves (Eder, 1989; Eder, Gerlach, & Perlmutter, 1987). The development of friendships in young children provides the opportunity of enhancing interpersonal sensitivity, social reasoning, and conflict-resolution skills (Volling, Youngblade, & Belsky, 1997).

There is a general tendency for children to form same-sex friendship groups that continues into adolescence (Bukowski, Gauze, Hoza, & Newcomb, 1993). Further, early school-age girls seem to enjoy more dyadic relationships whereas boys appear to enjoy larger groups (Benenson, 1993). These preferences are interesting in that they provide models for adult social relationships, where the dyad is associated with intimacy between partners and parent-child relationships, and the peer group is associated with teams, work groups, and families (Newman & Newman, 1999).

As children grow older, through their school years, they develop increasing dependence on the peer group as the primary influence in their lives. Parental influence diminishes greatly until, by early adolescence, teenagers may disregard it almost entirely. The need for friendship becomes so central to a young person's sense of self that not having friends may be unbearable and leads some children and adolescents to suicidal ideation, intent, and action.

> Ellen had always felt a little out of step with the other kids at school. She was not one of the popular kids, or a brainiac, or a jock; she was "just" Ellen. As she started her freshman year, she had a hard time adjusting to a new school and to the much bigger student population, and she felt increasingly isolated. One day, an older male student made fun of her clothes (which Ellen had considered part of her unique "style"). For the rest of the day she brooded about what had happened and, that night, cut her left wrist. Her parents found her unconscious and rushed her to the emergency room. She was later placed on an involuntary hold at a local psychiatric hospital. Upon release she came to my office for assessment and treatment.

Parents and teachers sometimes go to great lengths to ensure that the child is included in peer relationships. At home, a parent may invite other children over to play or may insist that their child attend birthday parties, bowling events, and so on. At school, teachers may force other children to play with a particularly isolated child. Often teachers or parents will observe that some children do not have any playmates. They may notice that the child is isolated at home or at school. Sometimes, these children are picked on or bullied by others. Sometimes they are simply ignored. These parents often seek treatment for their children. Teachers may make referrals for mental health services for children whom they identify as being at risk due to their lack of social skills or connections. In developing a treatment plan for children who have few friends, it is important to consider the referral source and the referral question.

> Alfred's mother brought him to my office. She said that Alfred was "too smart for his own good." She was right. Alfred was so smart that I had trouble keeping up with the topics he chose to discuss. He enjoyed casually talking about subjects as complex as astrophysics. Alfred was in the third grade. He no longer had any friends because, while his friends were looking for worms under trees at recess, Alfred preferred to ponder loftier issues. His former friends mostly ignored him now. Alfred was "okay" with being left alone because he thought his friends were "kind of dumb."

The first question that the mental health professional must ask in facing this type of situation is, "Whose problem is this?" Sometimes, the answer is that it is the parent's or the teacher's problem. That is, the adults worry so much about the child's asocial existence that they try to force socialization. The child may be unhappy or content in this situation, depending on personality. As treatment providers, clinicians first need to determine if the treatment plan is for the benefit of the child, the parent, or another interested adult.

If the answer to that question is the adult, then we need to let such adults know that their efforts on behalf of the child are appreciated and that they need to allow the child to develop problem-solving strategies, including socialization skills that will encourage more friendships. Perhaps the adult can be helped to work with the child to develop such strategies without micromanaging the process. If the answer to that question is the child, then a treatment plan can be developed together with the child, the parents, and any other interested party.

The second question that needs to be asked regarding a child with too few friends is, "Is this problem due to a lack of social skills, lack of social opportunities, or lack of interest?"

If the answer is lack of social skills, then children can be provided with information about good social skills and given opportunities to practice socialization. The information can be about what constitutes appropriate social functioning (such as telling the truth, taking turns, politeness, and interest in others) as well as behaviors that predict the potential for social ostracism (such as nose picking, foul smells, odd facial expressions, and peculiar sounds).

> Paul was in the fifth grade when his father brought him to me for treatment. Paul's few friends were social outcasts at the school. The small "band of brothers" had fun, although mostly outside of school. They would get together after school or on the weekend primarily because Paul's father orchestrated these meetings to make sure that Paul had some friends. When I asked Paul why he thought the kids at school did not like him or why even some of his friends excluded him from their parties, he graphically described his behaviors when in the company of others. These behaviors included making weird noises with his mouth, his nose, and other orifices. Paul also purposefully emitted foul smells, yawned in a bizarre manner that distorted his face, and engaged in other odd behaviors.

If the answer is lack of social opportunities, specific plans can be developed such as inviting a friend to the house or on vacation, or having a study partner. The more specific the plan, the more likely a positive outcome will be achieved.

If the answer is lack of interest, the therapist can inquire about attachment issues, that is, whether the lack of connection is isolated to peer relationships or extends to other aspects of the individual's social functioning, such as the family, school, teachers, or church. The answers to these inquiries will provide clues to what type of treatment planning is necessary.

Some children have severe deficits in socialization for a huge range of reasons including traumatic childhood events, ongoing trauma, genetic predisposition to depression or anxiety, learning deficits, giftedness, autism spectrum disorders, and so on. The therapist developing a treatment plan should explore all possibilities with the child, the parents, and other interested adults.

Most treatment plans for children with socialization problems include involvement in social skills development groups. Appropriate placement in such groups is essential. Treatment providers need to be sensitive to the impact of placement of children in such groups and the appropriateness of the groups in terms of age and gender, as well as the reasons for place-ment. When considering placement, ensuring that the individual will not be significantly deviant (in terms of age or ability to engage in the purpose of the group) is a primary consideration. An individual who is placed in a group that does not seem to fit his needs will likely drop out. Dropping out may cause additional problems for the individual and, incidentally, for the group. The individual will feel as if he failed in yet another group. The group members will wonder whether the group is a safe place to be or may feel devalued.

Many of the same considerations regarding asocial children apply to adults who have limited socialization. The difference is that adults with few friends have been dealing with this issue over a longer period of time. They have likely developed or cemented a negative view of themselves based on lack of connection.

With adults, therapists also have to ask if the individual is content with the status quo or desires change. Since adults normally are not mandated into treatment, except for legal issues or as recommended by influential adults, the adult in treatment will often be very unhappy. Adults who are satisfied with an asocial existence generally do not seek treatment, unless they develop psychological symptoms or behavioral manifestations that are caused by this limited interpersonal functioning. This category of adult may include hermits or people with certain diagnosable personality condi-tions, such as schizoid personality disorder.

> Cassandra sought treatment because she was having severe panic attacks and becoming increasingly depressed. Her affective state was beginning to impact her health and work. Assessment revealed that she had been ne-glected by both her mother and father, had been beaten repeatedly and brutally by her stepfather, and had been sexually molested by an adolescent stepbrother by the time she was in the third grade. She had engaged in many superficial friendships throughout high school and had been popular, yet had lacked any true friends. As an adult, Cassie developed a wonderful sense of empathy for the needy and helped many people who were home-less. She never told anybody about her sordid past—she was ashamed of what had happened to her and felt that it had been her fault—and never let anyone get close enough to know her "secret." Cassie was sure that if others knew about her past, they would judge her as she judged herself.

Sometimes, children, adolescents, and adults seek treatment because they are too involved in their social relationships. They may persistently overvalue others and devalue themselves. They may need the peer group's favor so much that they are willing to do things that they normally would not do, or they may give gifts to court the favor of others. They never express their needs, or they lose their sense of self through involvement with others.

In these situations, treatment plans need to assist the person to individuate and become more autonomous by highlighting the value of each individual regardless of the approval of others. Often, such individuals need to develop the skill of speaking up for what they want. They also need to learn to say no to others and yes to themselves. These are skills and concepts that can be taught and practiced within the therapy setting, with the therapist role-playing the part of the person with whom the client needs to practice. Ideally, individuals can then generalize the skills learned in therapy and translate those skills into their everyday life. The therapist can reinforce clients when they have tried and succeeded. When clients try a new behavior and fail, the therapist can emphasize the fact that they made an effort. The therapist should remind the client, "Practice makes better." Therapists reinforce successes and failures in a similar fashion: by providing a cognitive road map for understanding and illuminating the reasons for the client's successes and pointing them toward continued utilization of those positive skills despite any failures.

Willingness to Engage in Romantic Intimacy

Adults frequently seek professional services because of difficulties in intimate romantic and sexual relationships. Some people are afraid of intimacy because, at its core, intimacy places individuals in harm's way. The definition of intimacy is "a close, familiar, and usually affectionate or loving relationship with another person or group" (*Webster's*, 2001). This definition does not sound threatening.

However, intimacy can be pronounced "into-me-see." Other parts of the dictionary definition cite "closeness, inmost and essential essence." In fact, the phrase "intimate apparel" refers to items of clothing that are worn next to the skin and hidden under outer garments. Sometimes, we desire to hide who we really are and are threatened by exposure.

It follows that some people have difficulties with intimacy because to engage in intimate relations with another requires revealing oneself and becoming vulnerable to the judgments of others. This vulnerability applies, to varying degrees, to the full spectrum of intimacy, including friendships, romantic connections, and sexual intimacy.

Cassie had married when she was a teenager as a means of escaping the daily horror she experienced at the hands of her stepfather and stepbrother (mentioned above). But her husband was demanding and insensitive to her feelings. He pressured her into forced sexual behavior without consideration of her needs or desires. Cassie would always acquiesce, because she did not want to lose the only adult relationship that she had ever allowed herself to have. The marriage had lasted for years, but the apparent stability of it came at the cost of Cassie's self-respect and increasing psychological symptoms.

Treatment planning for adults who have never engaged in intimate relationships with others and are unhappy about that reality requires delving into the individual's entire psychosocial and psychosexual history to understand what the person has learned about the meaning of intimacy. Also, a thorough evaluation of the client's present interpersonal functioning will be helpful in assessing current strengths and weaknesses. Finally, the evaluator must determine exactly what the individual desires. The more precise one can be about future goals, the better chance of achieving such goals. Remember that a treatment plan is primarily the establishment of SMART (specific, measurable, attainable, realistic, and time limited) goals that an individual chooses to achieve.

Therapists believe that the most common reasons for failure to commit to intimate connection with others are fear and anxiety. Common fears include the anticipation that the love extended will not be reciprocated, that the other person might take advantage of us, and that, if the other person actually learns all about us, they will not like us. Such fears may be based on outcomes of past interpersonal and intimate relationships, including friendships. These beliefs may also go as far back in personal history as difficulties with attachment to primary care providers in infancy. As previously discussed, difficulties with attachment affect how we think and feel about ourselves. That sense of self will temper our willingness to allow ourselves to be fully known by others. Attachment issues also affect how safe we believe our environment is, including how trustworthy we deem others to be.

After careful assessment of the various potential factors for adults who fail to commit to intimate relationships, a treatment plan can be developed with clients who want something better for themselves. That plan must take into account the desires and aspirations of clients regarding intimate connection as well as their values, goals, and dreams for the future.

Many treatment plans on the topic of intimate connection and sexual experience will require extensive psychotherapy to help individuals deal with the demons of their past. These treatment plans involve goals for helping people learn to trust and to risk. These aspects of intimacy tend to be difficult to change because they have been part of the person's understanding of self and others for a protracted period of time. People need to expel the poisons before they can heal. Most treatment plans will help individuals modify the way they think and feel about themselves and about others. Treatment plans also need to include behavioral interventions in order to effect change. These plans should specify behaviors to initiate and engage in as well as behaviors to refrain from or curtail.

Besides fear of involvement in romantic or sexual relationships, some people seek treatment because they too frequently and easily slide into romantic adventures and find themselves hurt or hurting others. Examples include people who engage in promiscuous sexual behavior despite the possibility of being discovered and suffering negative marital, vocational, medical, or legal problems. For some, promiscuity borders on addiction and is generally considered to be self-destructive. Frequently, individuals who engage in these behaviors are treated through 12-step programs that focus specifically on addictive sexual behaviors.

A common way to explore the meaning of this type of behavior is the A-B-C model, which looks at antecedents, behaviors, and consequences:

1. Antecedents may be recent or historical.
2. Behavior involves the actual activity that is the reason for seeking treatment.
3. Consequences refer to the positive and negative outcomes of said behavior.

Utilizing this A-B-C approach to understand behavior helps in the development of a treatment plan. The focus of these treatment plans should be on positive behaviors that the individual wants to increase that will compete with the negative behaviors that the individual chooses to eliminate or diminish. Helping individuals understand the full range of antecedents and consequences for a particular behavior is one way of helping clients determine their goals. Once specific relationship goals are established, practical interventions can be identified to achieve these goals.

Treatment planning for multiple and ill-advised intimate involvements must identify specific goals that clients choose to develop for themselves. Because this area is highly value laden, mental health professionals must be careful not to impose their values on the people they treat, except in the case of illegal behaviors, such as illegal sexual behavior with minors. Another exception is behaviors that are evidently counterproductive to the individual's stated goals, value system, or healthy well-being. In these situations, the therapist can assist clients to be clear about whether they choose to be involved in said behaviors or not. Ultimately, clients are customers (or, consumers of services) and they make decisions about their lives. The therapist's role is to remain concerned, accepting (nonjudgmental), genuine, and empathic. The responsibility for change remains with the client.

Parenting Skills

Parents come for services, whether psychotherapy or education, because they recognize their own deficits in parenting skills or because someone else has recognized these deficits (such as in the case of neglect or abuse of children) and has mandated them to receive services.

> Erin was strongly encouraged to see a therapist because her adolescent daughter was in danger of failing her junior year in high school. Her daughter did not complete her homework, talked back to teachers using foul language, and was repeatedly absent from school. Erin was a single parent, worked hard, and had a good job that allowed her a comfortable living. She recounted how her daughter was rude to her, did not follow any rules, and was generally out of her control. I asked Erin what her daughter valued most in life, so that I could determine what consequences she might impose on her daughter for misbehavior. Erin advised me that her daughter owned seemingly hundreds of pairs of shoes, and that these shoes were her prize possessions. When I asked Erin about confiscating her daughter's favorite shoes for a short period of time as a possible consequence, Erin was appalled. She said, "I can't do that. Her shoes are her life! I would be a bad mother if I did that."

The Family Wellness model was developed expressly for the purpose of assisting individuals and families by developing parenting and relationship skills that enhance the safety and well-being of everyone in the family. Parents are told to be leaders and models. Children are told that they are valuable and important in their families. Adults are shown the importance of being individuals and knowing how to connect with others, especially in intimate relationships. Other areas covered in the Family Wellness curriculum include the importance of dealing with change over the life span of the individual and the family, learning how to solve family problems, and learning how parents pass on values to their children and how children can talk with parents about value-laden topics.

Psychoeducational classes, such as Family Wellness: Survival Skills for Healthy Families, help individuals to develop parenting skills. Many other excellent parent education and family enrichment curricula are utilized by social service and nonprofit agencies, programs, and individual treatment providers. Treatment planning for inadequate parenting skills normally focuses on identifying resources for parenting, which may include counseling services, psychoeducational classes, parenting-focused Web sites, and books or magazines. Many such resources are available and mental health professionals need to stay abreast of national and local programs that are offered in their communities so that referrals can be made and families can benefit from these options.

Besides referral to resources, some individuals require additional treatment regarding their difficulties with attachment or deficits in meeting their own children's affective needs. Such work requires additional assessment and treatment planning to identify goals that will exactly define the deficits involved as well as the strengths exhibited by the person seeking services.

> Bob was an alcoholic who had been sober for 12 years. He was married but the marriage was "on the rocks." Bob wanted help with his preteen son after catching his son smoking cigarettes and drinking beer in the garage. Bob also suspected that his son had recently smoked marijuana. Upon assessment questioning, Bob spoke about his lifelong addiction problem. He revealed that his mother was also an alcoholic and that she had put whiskey in his baby bottle because she thought it was "cute." He said that he had never known his father, a soldier with whom his mother had had a "one-night stand" after both had apparently had too much to drink. Bob admitted that he had no emotional connection to his mother (except, perhaps, for feelings of hatred and disdain), and that he did not know how to be a father. He did not know if he wanted a relationship with his aging mother, but he knew that he wanted to be a better father than his own father had been.

The Family Wellness model is a strength-based program that allows practitioners to choose to focus on individual strengths while not ignoring deficits. The model posits that "what is focused on grows." Therefore, it is more beneficial for both therapists and clients to focus on the strengths that clients exhibit. While there are many negative elements that Bob revealed when he discussed his family of origin and marital life, the amazing part of Bob's story is that Bob wanted to be a better father, to break the chain of neglect. What an opportunity! When clients focus on their strengths and practice positive pro-social skills, there is less time to engage in negative, counterproductive behaviors.

INTERVENTIONS: THE NUTS AND BOLTS OF CONNECTION

The sound assessment of an individual, couple, or family leads to relevant treatment planning. Treatment plans identify goals that call for practical interventions to assist people in understanding their current reality, pointing them toward choices that will improve their lives and achieve their stated goals. This process ends in attitudinal and behavioral changes that result in improved personal and interpersonal relationships.

We have identified three areas in interpersonal functioning that potentially reflect strengths (or problems) with connection: the capacity for friendship, willingness to engage in romantic intimacy, and parenting skills.

The Capacity for Friendship

Friendship is an intimate encounter with another person that results from the ability to trust and the capacity to risk. When people develop a sense of trust with one another, they are more likely to be willing to reveal personal aspects of themselves that few people know. In that process, they make themselves vulnerable. When people choose to reveal themselves and to be seen by others, they are risking that they will not be liked, that others will use that private information against them, that they will be abandoned, or that they will be hurt in some other way. Conversely, these same people are risking the development of deep friendship that can be both a curative and a protective factor against depression, loneliness, isolation, and other negative outcomes of being alone.

> Cassie finally opened up to the therapist and revealed her "secret" of being neglected, beaten, and sexually abused repeatedly before she had reached the third grade [as described above]. Her original treatment plan was designed to reduce her panic attacks and make her happier. As she began to feel safer in the therapeutic environment and relationship, Cassie slowly revealed more aspects of her past. To her surprise, the world did not stop, she did not die, and the sun still shone. In fact, through cognitive-

behavioral interventions highlighting her patterns of thinking, feeling, and acting, Cassie noticed that her panic attacks remitted and she began to feel happy.

As these changes occurred, the treatment plan was modified by mutual consent to include issues such as forgiveness and reconciliation (with herself and others), as well as trust and risk. The plan emphasized the three skills necessary for healthy functioning: speaking, listening, and cooperating. Cassie was given opportunities to practice these skills within the therapy setting and was asked to journal about her thoughts, feelings, and actions. She is now carefully stepping out into the foreign (and terrifying) territory of true friendship, beginning to develop relationships with a neighbor and a coworker. She is risking connection.

Healthy friendships have been described as "good medicine." Friendships that go awry or are never actually reciprocal can be poisonous. An individual's willingness to engage in the development of friendship generally has its roots in either attachment to parents or the outcome of prior efforts at friendship.

Some psychotherapists spend a great deal of time exploring an individual's attachment to care providers and delving into that person's history of intimacy. That is time well spent and can provide a great deal of information. Some therapists, however, spend all of their time in treatment helping people understand themselves (providing insight) without ever engaging their clients in more active interventions. As a result, psychotherapy can become protracted and may not yield fully satisfactory outcomes. Such clients may attain significantly greater insights into their condition or behavior but may not actually achieve the outcomes or the behavioral changes they seek.

> The original treatment plan for Bob [introduced earlier] included material on how to be a leader and model for his son. He completed a Family Wellness workbook designed to help him understand his role as a parent. However, it became clear that he also needed to understand and repair his internal representations of what it meant to be a son and a father. Bob's treatment plan was adjusted to help him develop a realistic and positive sense of self, as well as make sense of his relationship with his mother, his father, his son, himself, and alcohol.

The Family Wellness practitioner believes that better results occur in psychotherapy when a person obtains information (insight) that leads to an affective response, which then results in an attitudinal or behavioral change. A concept borrowed from Franz Alexander to describe psychoanalytic cure is the *corrective emotional experience*. Franz Alexander's basic concept for helping effect true change is that patients must be exposed to experiences that previously had traumatic outcomes and be provided with opportunities (via new skills) to effect different emotional outcomes (Alexander & French, 1946).

The corrective emotional experience includes three components:

1. Insight alone is insufficient for change to occur.
2. A deep emotional response is required.
3. Systematic reality testing is necessary for change to stick.

The first important concept undergirding the corrective emotional experience is that intellectual insight alone is insufficient to effect change. Insight alone never cured anyone. Many people know that they need to change some important aspect of themselves. They could desire to lose weight, to exercise more, to cease certain counterproductive behaviors, or to start some other action. Awareness alone does not result in change. Insight is important, but it is not sufficient.

The second important concept is that people must experience the need for and possibility of change at an emotional level. It is not enough for people to have an intellectual understanding of the need for and the possibility of change; they must feel deeply about the issue. They need to get it at a gut level. In Alexander's construct, people must actually re-experience, under more favorable circumstances, interpersonal dynamics that previously produced difficult emotional outcomes and now have different results. This re-experience can be simulated in the counseling office individually or in a group process, and then practiced in real life.

Some people choose to change due to an insight and they have strong feelings about wanting to change. They may even make a conscious decision to change, an act of will. Nevertheless, they fail to change. This scenario is often played out in New Year's Eve resolutions, such as when we vow to exercise more, drink less, or make some other significant change. Within a few days or weeks into the New Year, we are often doing the things we vowed not to do and are not doing the things that we wanted to do. The decision to change is important, yet also insufficient.

The third requirement for a corrective emotional experience is systematic reality testing (Yalom & Leszcz, 2005), which means that people must obtain information and have experiences that challenge their presumptions about self and others (which are both usually negative). Through these reality checks, a person begins to recognize that past experiences and the resulting internalized images may no longer apply in the current situation. This reality testing may help the individual come to recognize that change is both desirable and possible. The therapist is responsible for creating learning and experiencing environments in which clients can have new insights, develop new affective connections, and begin to see themselves in a new light.

Ultimately, change at a behavioral level and at a deeper level of internalized images occurs as a result of meaningful here-and-now relational experience that disconfirms prior erroneous beliefs about self and others (Fonagy, Moran, Edgcumbe, Kennedy, & Target, 1993; Weiss, 1993). When an individual acts in a new way and the feared catastrophic events do not occur, the new reality forms a positive feedback loop that allows the person to explore other new behaviors that were previously avoided and not enacted due to fear of vulnerability.

The experiences and interventions that the Family Wellness model uses to help individuals and families engage in previously feared behaviors involve role-play, sculpting, and group experiences.

Role-play in a therapy office is similar to the empty chair technique in Gestalt therapy, where the individual is asked to imagine a person sitting in an empty chair and to talk directly to that person. The twist is that the therapist or another family member in the room can play the part of the other person with whom the client has chosen to speak.

In developing a role-play scenario, it is important for the therapist to obtain as much information about that other person as possible in order to enact the role in a similar manner to how that person would likely respond.

This type of intervention is very useful because an individual can be coached to say things that were not previously said or to say things in a different way. This acting or reenactment process allows clients to practice communication skills that may have been lacking in the past. This is done in the safety of the therapy room, which results in an excellent opportunity to experience positive outcomes in previously fear-laden interactions. Once clients are able to practice these skills adequately in the therapy room, they are asked to generalize these new skills in their real world.

Ellen, the high school freshman who attempted suicide in part due to social insecurities [described above], can be helped to practice saying what she wants and needs in certain situations that normally cause her anxiety. She can practice her communications skills with the therapist, who then can ask her to practice speaking with others. Naturally, a treatment plan for anyone who is at risk of suicidal ideation or behavior needs to include safety plans, such as contracting for safety. Interventions involving behaviors that have a good chance of successful completion are ideal, because individuals who become suicidal have usually lost hope. Clients who have developed such severe depression will also likely require psychopharmacological intervention, which is a delicate topic for someone who has made efforts at self-harm. Such individuals require monitoring and support. Often the entire family needs to be involved to help the individual develop hope in self, in others, and in the future.

Sculpting is the physical placement of individuals in the therapy room in ways that simulate how they are feeling in relationship to others. If people feel close to one another, they are placed close together in a family therapy session. If they feel distant, they are placed as far apart in the room as possible. A person who feels less than or superior to someone else would be asked to sit on the ground or on a chair or to stand on a chair. Such physical placements result in visceral responses in individuals in a way that does not occur by simply talking about how one feels in relationship to others. If only one person is in the room, that person is asked to simulate the others based on distance from a chair or other furniture in the room and to visualize those objects as people important in his or her life. Moving closer to or further from another, as well as standing above or sitting below another, are ways of helping people sense their connection or lack of connection with others. Other sculpting interventions include crossing arms, opening arms to varying degrees, holding hands, or standing beside, behind, ahead of, or back to back. Each of these positions evokes a different affective response and provides insight. The cognitive and affective evocations also strengthen the resolve to change.

Group experiences involve a variety of interventions including the development of problem-solving dyads or group experiences. In these small groups, assuming a family or multifamily meeting, people are asked to group themselves into dyads or other small groups and to focus on solving specific problems by using prescribed strategies. It is often helpful to complete the problem-solving process either on a piece of paper that has the problem-solving steps written on it or by writing on a very large poster board when the groups proceed through the problem-solving steps one at a time. The problem-solving strategies are identical to the Family Wellness treatment plan previously described:

- What is the presenting or primary issue?
- What is the desired outcome?
- Who is needed to solve the problem?
- Brainstorm solutions.
- Choose the solution to implement.
- Who does what by when?

Once solutions are identified, these smaller groups may then share their strategies and outcomes with the larger group. Engaging in such a process can help individuals develop a sense of competency that can be generalized to solving other problems in life.

When focusing interventions on an individual's capacity for friendship, clinicians are usually talking to just one person in the therapy setting. Thus, some of the interventions described above may not apply in a therapy room setting but definitely do apply in psychoeducational classes. These practical interventions can be modified to meet the need for more people, such as through the use of inanimate objects found in the office, or by the therapist role-playing, or through imagining other people.

Regarding friendship interventions, practitioners are usually dealing with people in one of three categories: individuals who do not know how to engage in friendship, people who are afraid to engage in friendship, or people who may be in enmeshed friendship relationships. Interventions will vary based on the individual's need.

People who do not know how to engage in friendship either want more friendships or do not want social connection. The individuals who do not want social connection are generally not in our therapy offices. They do not seek outside help because they do not feel that they are missing anything by not having friendships.

Individuals who do want friendships often seek therapy due to a profound sense of isolation, depression, or anxiety. The most practical thing we can do with these individuals is give them socialization skills that they can practice in the room and that they can later generalize in their actual lives.

In the therapy room, the process of social interaction can be normalized by explaining that the therapeutic relationship is one kind of social interaction. By simply being in the therapist's office, the person is already using skills necessary for social interactions. Clients have made an appointment (or allowed someone to make an appointment on their behalf) and kept the appointment. They will likely have introduced themselves and provided some information to help the therapist understand the reasons for the appointment. These factors are highlighted to identify some of the social skills clients already have. These skills form the foundation upon which additional skills can be developed. The Family Wellness practitioner always looks for what is working rather than for what is not working. Helping clients see what is working in their lives is the beginning of providing them with a new perspective on self. It helps create within clients a sense of ability instead of disability.

Some people need very basic information about appropriate interpersonal behavior. For them, a step-by-step discussion about core skills followed by practice of the skills of speaking, listening, and problem solving can be extremely helpful. The therapist may highlight how the skills are involved in the process of making an appointment, keeping it, interacting in the therapy office, and what the person does after a therapy session. This discussion can be extremely useful. This process normalizes the experience of socialization and makes it less threatening. It also highlights the fact that the individual has already been successful at least in procuring and initiating a professional relationship. The therapist can then have an interactive discussion about how the client can use the same skills in other social interactions. Such individuals need social skills development through information and practice.

Other clients may fully understand the process of socialization but may not successfully engage in it due to either depression or anxiety, or both. They may have had negative experiences in the past when they tried to develop friendships and got stuck in an attitude of learned helplessness. If people already have information about how to socialize, they need practice. Treatment plans will call for interventions related to engaging the person in real-world social experiences.

These individuals may be asked to ride the bus, the subway, or the train or engage in other situations where at least some socialization can be practiced. The clinician can ask about the social groups in which the client already participates. Clients are asked to return to the office and discuss their practice experiences in the community and in groups. The therapist will reinforce any positive experiences. The therapist will reframe any negative experiences to include the fact that the person at least made an effort, even if the outcome was negative. In some cases, the client may have thought about engaging in the behavior but did not actually do it. In such situations, the fact that the client thought about it is deemed as the first step to actually making it happen. Remember, what we focus on

grows. The therapist can work with the client to fine tune the desired behaviors and can send the client out to practice the newly tuned skills. The
process is repeated until the client has successful outcomes. Always make
the goals small enough to enhance the likelihood of success. Build on the
client's experiences of success.

Willingness to Engage in Romantic Intimacy

Love is a many-splendored thing—for most people. For some, love is a
vexing type of connection that is perennially lacking or, at the other extreme, becomes overwhelming because of its complexity and intrusive-
ness. Therapists treat people on the topic of romantic or sexual intimacy
for three major reasons along a continuum from too little love to too much
love.

First, some people have not found love. They desire to love and to be
loved yet have not found the right person. Angst grows over time as these
people become increasingly worried that they will never find Mr. or Ms.
Right.

Second, some people have found love yet they are unsure about the
nature of that love relationship. They are unsure if their partner wants to
continue in that relationship so they may become highly possessive, controlling, or jealous. Others are not sure whether they want to continue the
relationship. This is often the case when clients tell the therapist, "I love
my partner, but I'm not *in love* with my partner."

Third, some people keep falling in love or lust over and over. These
people love being in love. They usually come to the therapist's office because someone advises them that their affection is their affliction. Someone sets a boundary with them or they get into some sort of trouble. They
often face significant negative consequences for their adventures and mis-
adventures in love.

For individuals who have not found love, the therapist may offer the
following counsel: Not everyone has to fall in love. Not everyone has to
experience sexuality. There are people who choose to love an ideal, who
have a passion for something grander than themselves, something transcendent. These people can find fulfillment through the investment of
their lives in something meaningful to them. Often, they and society benefit from their choices in life. People who choose either the single life or
chastity often channel their time and energy into pro-social endeavors.

Nevertheless, most people desire to fall in love, to commit to a relationship, and to possibly build a family. Individuals who have these aspirations become anxious when their goals are not being reached on their timetable.

Today, many people delay making any commitments to marriage or similar relationships because of competing goals, such as completing an education, developing a career, or becoming financially stable. Therefore, many people are single for a longer period of time than was typical historically. The longer people remain single, the more entrenched they become in their patterns of behavior. The older people get while being single, the higher the expectations become for the ideal partner and the harder it is to share certain aspects of life, such as time, space, and decision making. Given these realities, there may be fewer acceptable romantic partners and less willingness to settle.

Yet many people genuinely desire to meet someone whom they can love and respect. When prospects of finding such a partner begin to dim, some people begin to look for love in all the wrong places. Others seek professional counseling.

The best interventions for individuals who seek love and romance are to help them take personal inventory of themselves in order to gain an appreciation for their strengths and weaknesses. The Family Wellness model encourages people to be Mr. or Ms. Right rather than seeking to find Mr. or Ms. Right.

In appreciating ourselves and choosing to focus on our strengths, we begin to recognize our worth and value. In relationships, emotionally healthy people tend to attract other healthy people. People who value themselves will feel better than people who focus on their failings. People who value themselves will likely make good choices in many areas of their lives, such as how they care for themselves, what they eat, the amount of exercise they get, and in their friendship and love relationships. People who have a realistic and positive sense of self often are able to translate their love of self into love of others, expending energy in humanitarian or other pro-social behaviors.

A second category of individuals who seek relationship counseling consists of those who are in a committed relationship but are not committed to it. They are unsure about the commitment of the other person in the relationship or about their own commitment. For such individuals, the ideal intervention involves helping clients to know what they want and to say what they want, which will give them the best chance of getting what they want. That simple three-part outline can be very profound in terms of helping people maneuver through this very difficult situation.

Adrianna and her husband, Pete, came to my office for marriage counseling. She told me that Pete was an alcoholic and that she was not sure if she wanted to continue her relationship with him. She said that two years ago Pete had suddenly announced that he knew he had to change. He had gone into a drug and alcohol rehabilitation program and stopped drinking altogether. Arianna lamented, "The day Pete went into rehab was the worst day of my life!" She explained that although she did not like Pete drinking too much, she liked going to parties. After rehab, they no longer went to those parties.

The hardest part of this outline is the first part: know what you want. People will often tell you what they do not want, saying things like, "I do not want to stay in my marriage the way it is" or "I don't want my husband to drink too much." Therapists can help people focus on what they do want, instead of simply what they do not want. The intervention for Adrianna was to remove her from marriage counseling and engage her in individual counseling, so that she could determine if she wanted to continue the former. The line of questioning was "If you are not sure you want to continue, tell me what you are sure about." That open-ended inquiry can help a person begin to determine what they want instead of being unsure or focusing on what they do not want.

When people are prompted to say what they want, they generally become very vague: For example, "I want to be happier" or "I want to be at peace." The therapist's primary job here is to help clients become extremely specific about what they want. Think of a funnel, which is wide at the top and very narrow at the bottom. The therapist's job is to help people become increasingly specific about what they want. If we are successful, our clients will be in a better position to proactively pursue their newly and more precisely defined goals.

Once people know what they want, they need to be able to communicate it effectively to others. This task is accomplished by using the skill of speaking up. As easy as that sounds, there are many people who do not know how to communicate their thoughts, desires, hopes, and feelings in a way that provides the best opportunity for others to actually hear and understand them. Speaking up is discussed in greater detail in Chapter 3. For now, it is important to remember to start this form of communication with the word "I," to make statements instead of asking questions, and to be as specific as possible.

In order for people to have the best chance of getting what they want, they need to both know what they want and to say so. However, even when people know what they want and say it effectively, they do not always get what they want. For individuals to have the best chance of actually getting what they want, they need to know how to cooperate and negotiate well.

The basic attitude behind negotiation is the skill of cooperation. The question that the therapist needs to ask in order to give clients the best chance of getting what they want is, "What are you willing to do to get what you want?" Negotiating effectively in intimate interpersonal relationships involves seeking to get a good deal for oneself and for the other person involved. In other words, the optimal outcome is a win-win, where each person in the relationship is fulfilled. For example, to expect to always get only what I want is selfish, especially if I only think about my needs being fulfilled. To never get what I want results in frustration and creates distance in a relationship. To use speaking and listening skills while continuing to negotiate provides the best possible outcome in resolving conflict. Such an outcome also increases the intimacy connection between the two people involved because each person is assured that no matter how much discord exists, trust develops that the other person will still be there after the dust settles.

The therapist helps people who are unclear about their own commitment by asking questions that help them clarify what they want in their current relationship. The therapist helps people who are unsure about the level of commitment of the other person in the relationship by teaching them to develop and practice their listening skills.

People who are insecure in a given relationship may have problems due to attachment issues in infancy. However, they may also be insecure in the relationship because their partner is, in fact, cheating on them. The old saying is, "It ain't paranoia if they're really after you." Discerning the difference between these disparate situations involves helping clients to develop their listening skills. Clients can learn to listen to words, emotions, and energy levels. They can also learn to listen to nonverbal communications. Individuals in this situation need to learn to understand themselves well in order to differentiate between a partner who is trustworthy and one who is not. It is not healthy to trust someone who is not trustworthy. Wisdom is, in part, learning to read the cues and knowing the difference between those who are trustworthy and those who are not.

The third category of individuals who seek therapy for difficulties with connection is those who fall in love repeatedly, who act on their affections, and whose lives become significantly complicated. These individuals often have difficulties in establishing or maintaining boundaries in their romantic or sexual lives. At an extreme, their behavior can appear to be, and may actually become, addictive. There are many forms of treatment that deal with sexual acting-out as an addiction. Such individuals may be referred to clinical programs, self-help groups, or faith-based programs to help them deal with difficulties with fidelity. These programs often follow a 12-step model.

Addiction is defined simply as doing anything repeatedly despite knowing that engaging in the behavior will likely result in negative consequences. The etiology of addiction is undoubtedly multifaceted. How we think about the addiction, what treatment plan we will develop, and what interventions we will attempt all depend on which school of psychotherapy we have for our clinical worldview.

Like any other form of addiction, love and sex addictions are very difficult to change. Every addiction has a self-reinforcing aspect. Who doesn't want to be in love? Surprisingly, a large number of people with these addictions know that their behaviors are self-destructive and harm others. Nevertheless, they appear unable to change their behavior.

The most difficult aspect of working with a person who has an addiction is not getting the individual to decide to change. They often intellectually grasp the need for change. The most difficult aspect is getting clients to engage in interventions that work long enough for the behavior to change. Neural pathways that activate the pleasure centers in the brain become powerful forces for behavior. Even when behavioral change occurs, the new behavioral patterns are not deeply engrained because they have not been practiced for long. Stress can easily result in a return to previously learned behaviors that are powerfully reinforcing. Individuals engage in the negative behaviors even in the face of overwhelming negative potential, and actual, consequences. The old patterns or neural pathways are more comfortable, much like an old pair of shoes. New shoes may pinch and be uncomfortable. New behaviors, supportive of fidelity, need to be practiced for long periods of time before they become the new normal.

Successful treatment plans identify very specific goals for the client. These goals are developed by, or in conjunction with, the client. When individuals are involved in the development of goals, there is more buy-in and a willingness to engage in the difficult work necessary to be successful. The first therapeutic intervention is to help the individual determine what he or she actually wants. If several goals are identified, then the therapist must help the client identify the priorities, encouraging the client to "pick one." It is hard to accomplish several things at once. It is better to develop a hierarchy of what will be done and in what order.

Helping people acknowledge the worth and value of others in their lives (often a spouse and kids) is an important step in helping them determine who and what they want in their lives. Even after cognitive decisions for change have been made, behavioral change needs to occur and be reinforced.

If an individual is engaged in an extramarital romantic or sexual relationship and desires to salvage the marriage, the individual needs to cut off all contact with the other person. To fail to do so immediately will delude the person into thinking that he can continue to have it both ways, to have his cake and eat it too. Once people have recommitted to their marriage (or other committed relationship) they need to begin to build new memories.

Naturally, issues of forgiveness and reconciliation will need to be addressed. The offending party needs to ask for forgiveness in order to have a chance of reconciliation. To have a chance of receiving forgiveness, individuals need to recognize that they have done something wrong and accept responsibility. Most offenders resort to three ways of avoiding responsibility: They minimize, rationalize, and externalize.

To minimize is to believe or state that the offense was not as big as it is being made out to be. "After all," the person complains, "I have only done this a few times. I don't know why everyone is making such a big deal out of this."

To rationalize is to have very clear explanations for the behavior, none of which involve acknowledging personal guilt. Although these explanations often defy external logic, they make perfect sense to the person engaging in the rationalization. When such individuals consider why they broke marriage vows, for example, they are able to explain with great confidence, "Since we were married so young, it is expected and natural that we would become bored and seek outside comfort."

To externalize is to extend the rationalization. A client might say, "My spouse drove me to it through his [or her] behavior. Had he [she] only been more compassionate and understanding, I would not have been driven to do this." The externalization places all the blame on the other party. "I see now that it was actually my spouse's fault that I did what I did."

As therapists it is crucially important that we help people to accept responsibility for their behaviors. Failure to accept responsibility will lead to minimizing, rationalizing, and externalizing. These behaviors may work to deflect blame for a while. However, in the long run they will prevent any chance of reconciliation. Our interventions, therefore, have to focus on confronting these grand efforts at avoiding responsibility.

Parenting Skills

The good news about deficits in parenting skills is that parenting skills can be learned. The Family Wellness curriculum provides a simple way of thinking about the basic parenting tasks. While there are many excellent programs to which parents can be referred to improve their parenting skills, it is important that any program be culturally sensitive, be adaptable to diverse situations, be taught in everyday language, use a variety of teaching methods, and involve the whole family.

The basics of good parenting are relatively concrete. Parents are leaders and models. Parents lead their families by the kind of structure that they establish in the home. The rules are the frame of a healthy house. Some people have so many rules that the members of the family have no room for individuality or creativity. They feel suffocated. Too many rules, in the extreme, can lead to abuse. Some people have so few rules that the members of the family can do whatever they want, whenever they want. There is no clear definition of the entity known as family. Too few rules, in the extreme, can lead to neglect. The rules that parents establish for their families really represent their values in action.

Parents model for their family by the way they live their lives. Whether parents like it or not, children are always watching and learning from them. Unless they make a clear choice to do something else, children almost always grow up to be just like their parents. Healthy parents live their lives congruent with a set of values that they believe in and want their children to choose when they grow up. Healthy parents make time for their children, encourage their children, and listen to and talk together with their children.

These relatively simple concepts are known and well respected in most parent education programs and in the parenting literature. They can be easily learned via instruction in the therapy room, through reading parenting books or workbooks, or via referral to parenting programs in the community.

The principles described throughout this book form the basis of the Family Wellness model for parent education. Sometimes, it is useful to provide clients with a family workbook or other form of bibliotherapy in order to have the family work on developing communication skills or problem-solving strategies. The family members can report their progress to the therapist, who can monitor their abilities and provide feedback.

Even individuals who had difficult attachment relationships with primary care providers can develop families in which the basic requirements for attachment are promoted and practiced. For example, family members can learn to give and receive messages that demonstrate each person's worth and value within the family. This outcome is achieved by consistently using the basic skills of speaking, listening, and cooperating. The result of improving parenting skills is improved trust within the members of a family, an increased willingness to share of themselves and, therefore, an increase in the potential for interpersonal intimacy among family members.

SUMMARY

In Chapter 1 we learned the importance of having a realistic and positive sense of self for an individual's well-being: the development of a healthy Me. It is precisely that sense of worth and value that allows an individual to engage in the dangerous proposition of connecting with another individual to form a new entity, known as a relationship: the construction of a healthy We.

The delicate work of constructing a We involves the fear that if we are not strong enough, our individuality may be overwhelmed by the other and our self-identity may be lost. On the other hand, if I am too strong, the other person may lose his identity.

Some people are excellent at establishing relationships. Other people never establish healthy relationships. The ideal is that people should know how to find balance in their lives by having a strong sense of self and learning how to develop a strong connection with others. The Family Wellness model refers to these dual tasks as the two jobs of the individual.

In order to accomplish these two jobs successfully, all individuals need three foundational skills. The core skills for the Family Wellness model are the ability to speak, to listen, and to cooperate. These three skills are the subject of the next section.

SECTION II

THREE SKILLS

3

Speak

Be a Leader

Say what you mean. Mean what you say.

Old Adage

THE FAMILY WELLNESS model posits that the ability to speak up for oneself is one of three foundational skills necessary for an individual to be psychologically healthy. In most Western cultures, assertiveness is highly valued. To be assertive is defined as being "confidently aggressive or self-assured; positive; aggressive; dogmatic" (*Webster's*, 2001).

The ability to speak up for what we need and want is generally considered a sign of strength, a demonstration of leadership. People follow leaders. The adage is true: "If you want to know whether you are a leader, look behind you." When people say what they want, they reveal themselves and allow others to know them better. That act requires a great deal of self-confidence because to open up is to let others see who you really are, which involves a degree of risk. When an individual does not speak up, silence is deemed a sign of weakness, a demonstration of lack of confidence, and an abdication of a person's innate right be heard. Psychotherapists frequently treat individuals who do not give voice to their needs, who feel taken advantage of by others, and whose needs are not being met.

Some people do not speak up for what they need or want because they do not believe that it is safe to do so. They correctly equate opening up to becoming vulnerable. Imagine a person who has his arms crossed protec-

tively over his chest and who then opens his arms wide apart. Such an individual could get kicked in the stomach or otherwise be attacked. Many
people learn, when growing up, that people who show vulnerability can,
and often will, be hurt. If that is an individual's perspective, it makes sense
to be very cautious about speaking up. In fact, this cautiousness can become a pattern of guardedness that results in the person's needs consistently not being met. Further, such individuals may develop alternative
unhealthy patterns of interaction by which they attempt to meet their
needs. These behaviors then result in difficult interpersonal relationships.
Such conflicted relationships often bring people to the therapy office.

It is likely that the person who does not speak up will not get his or her
needs met, often simply because others do not know what the person
wants. Also, if a person consistently does not speak up, other people will.
The others will fill the vacuum. As a result, less and less of an individual's
needs will be known. That person may begin to believe that what he has
to say is not as important as what other people say. The individual begins
to either deny his own needs, subjugate his needs to the needs of others,
or assume that his needs are less important. Further, a person who does
not communicate directly with others may begin to develop indirect ways
of trying to get others to know his needs.

One example of indirect communication is known as passive-aggressive
behavior. We are upset that others do not know what we want (despite
our not having said what we want). We think, "If she really loved me, she
would know what I want." As a result of our frustration and anger, we behave in ways that demonstrate our feelings without actually saying what
those feelings are. We may not do what we said we were going to do, or
we may delay in complying with the requests of others. In either case, we
enact our emotions physically rather than saying how we feel. The nonverbal communication may be compensation for feelings of impotency, an
expression of anger, or an effort to control the other.

These passive-aggressive actions are often meant to punish the other
person for not reading our mind and heart. This is considered indirect
communication because we are unable or unwilling to talk directly to the
other person, sometimes for fear of their response or of possible retribu-
tion.

Lorenzo grew up in a tough part of town. He enjoyed school but did not
enjoy walking to high school. Daily, he was chased and coerced, by threats
of physical violence, out of his lunch money. He developed physical symp-

toms of anxiety, such as upset stomach, sweating, and general fear. He wished he could drop out of school. He never told his mother what was happening to him. He did not know his father and probably would not have told him anyway due to embarrassment. One day he realized that things had to change. He determined that he could not be scared his entire life. He decided that this was the day he was going to stand up for himself. As he walked to school, the bully approached him and demanded his money. Lorenzo told him that he would not give it up and that the bully was going to have to beat him up if he wanted the money. The bully beat him up and took the money, but he never bothered Lorenzo again.

By definition, a person who feels one-down (less powerful) in relationship to another normally cannot speak directly with the person in the one-up role, who may be considered an authority figure. Therefore, we defer to that person's judgment. In extreme cases, the one-up person may be considered a bully and we do not want to jeopardize our safety and well-being. So we do not speak up directly to that person. At any rate, the longer we stay in a one-down role with another person, the more entrenched both positions become.

In the 1980s, this one-up/one-down style of communication was a paradigm known as transactional analysis. The concept was that we need to communicate as adults yet we often take a one-down role (submissive child) or a one-up role (authoritarian parent). Healthy adults relate to one another as adults (equals). Healthy young people relate to other youths as equals.

The Family Wellness model translates these transactional analysis concepts into the construct of communicating from an above (leading), below (following), or beside (coequal) position (see Figure 2.3). Specifically, the model describes people practicing mature communication styles when they are able to place themselves in the communication stance (above, below, or beside) that is appropriate to the circumstance. We are appropriately below when we are dealing with people in authority, such as bosses or teachers. We are correctly above when we are fulfilling a task, such as parenting our children or in charge of a project. We seek to be in a side-by-side communication style when we are dealing with our spouse or a good friend.

Healthy people know how to identify the appropriate communication stance and practice it in any given interpersonal situation. Unhealthy people are either unable to correctly identify their role with respect to others, are unable to correctly appraise the role of the other person in a communication dyad, or do not have the skills to communicate effectively. The Family Wellness model provides a cognitive road map to help correctly identify one's appropriate level of communication in relationship to another, the other person's level, and the specific skills that provide for the best possibility of being an effective, assertive communicator. Psychotherapists who know how to quickly assess their client's level of assertiveness will be in a good position to determine how to effectively assist that individual in achieving his or her goals in life.

ASSESSMENT: TO SPEAK OR NOT TO SPEAK

The Family Wellness model asserts that the degree to which individuals speak up for themselves is directly related to their self-confidence and self-esteem. People who are assertive demonstrate a positive sense of self precisely because they speak up. They recognize that they have something of value to say. Speaking up in an assertive manner is one-third of what it takes for a person to be interpersonally mature. Another third is the capacity to listen to others. The final third is the ability to cooperate through a process of negotiation. Mental health professionals can assess an individual's level of assertiveness (speaking up) by listening carefully to the person's communication style. See Figure 3.1 for the Family Wellness Communication Matrix that the mental health professional can use to assess an individual's capacity to speak up.

Whether we are listening via clinical interview, formal assessment using a variety of testing instruments, or simply talking with an individual, it is possible to ascertain the frequency, tone, level, and directness of an individual's communications. The person who speaks up in an interpersonally mature manner is accepting responsibility for his thoughts, feelings, actions, and needs. He usually starts his sentences with the word "I" and demonstrates leadership. The person who does not speak up for himself is demonstrating the exact opposite. The reasons for failure to speak up may stem from idiosyncratic histories, but the results will normally be negative for each individual no matter the etiology. Before intervening in an effort to assist our clients, we must first accurately determine the individual's placement on an assertiveness continuum. This, then, becomes the predominant assessment task in determining an individual's ability to speak up.

The more frequent and direct an individual's statements (generally starting with the word "I"), the more likely it is that the individual is asser-

FIGURE 3.1
COMMUNICATION MATRIX

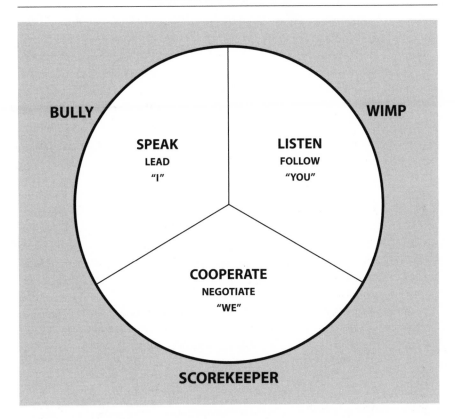

tive. Healthy assertiveness occurs over a continuum, from frequently speaking up for what is needed and wanted to rarely speaking up. There is no best measure of assertiveness, no specific location on such a continuum that is deemed optimal. Instead, assertiveness occurs over a range. People who are being assertive in a healthy manner let others know who they are and what they need.

It is also possible, however, to be so assertive that the person only speaks up and never listens to others. That person has moved on the continuum past high assertiveness into aggressiveness. This is an immature style of communicating. The reason Family Wellness refers to this style as immature is that, developmentally, toddlers, adolescents, and some adults deal with the world in an egocentric manner. They believe that the world revolves around them and their needs. They never, or rarely, listen to others because it is immaterial to them what other people need or desire. This way of being demonstrates that these people only care about their own needs and believe that others do not matter. Such an individual could be described as a bully.

Individuals may move past assertive to aggressive if they speak up so much that they overpower the person with whom they are communicating. In other words, they know how to speak up (which is healthy) but do not know how to listen to others (which is unhealthy). In that case, they have moved from a healthy assertive style to being aggressive and feeling entitled to speak without a concomitant sense of being required to listen. They position themselves, with respect to the other, in the above role whether or not that position is warranted. Even if they are actually in a position superior to others, that style of communication becomes counterproductive and the bully will likely be viewed with fear or disdain and will get only grudging cooperation, if that. It is a less than optimal communication style. A therapist's accurate assessment of this interactive style and the resultant skills-based practical interventions can change the person's life in a tremendously positive way.

> Jasmine, a successful attorney, knew exactly what she was going to be when she grew up. From her earliest years she was good at arguing her case and winning. Her parents called her "precocious." Her peers called her "bossy and a know-it-all." When she finished high school, she was voted most likely to succeed. She did. However, when Jasmine brought her highly successful aggressive courtroom style home and dealt with her husband in the same manner, she was highly unsuccessful, which is what brought her in for therapy.

Some people, like Jasmine, know how to be assertive from a young age. They may have seen assertiveness modeled by their parents; they may have had to be assertive (as when living in a large family); or assertiveness may simply be part of their personality. As they mature, these individuals continue to be assertive and also find ways of listening to others and incorporating the others' needs in order to find solutions that work. High assertiveness is an indicator of healthy interpersonal functioning, at least in Western societies where assertiveness is valued as a positive trait.

At the other end of the continuum, some people speak up for themselves so infrequently that they occupy a position no longer described as assertive. Instead, this point on the continuum is denoted as passive and is characterized by fear, retreat, and deference. Such individuals almost never speak up, primarily due to fear. This style of communicating is as immature as being a bully. It is immature because, for a variety of reasons, these individuals do not let others know who they are or what they need, yet they expect others to read their minds or hearts. An individual at this point on the continuum would be described as a wimp and has moved into a one-down role in relationship with others.

In the one-down position, individuals defer to other people's needs, are afraid to let people know where they stand, and become angry at others yet feel impotent to effect any change in their interpersonal dynamics. They may feel defeated and withdraw further from interpersonal relationships, confirming to themselves their one-down status.

Looking for evidence of healthy levels of assertiveness requires that therapists have finely tuned skills of listening and assessing. Our clients will show us their position on the assertiveness continuum if we are careful listeners. Our interpersonal functioning style, as therapists, becomes our best assessment instrument.

What therapists are listening for begins with how the individual relates to us. Part of that equation is how we therapists present ourselves to our clients. If we take a one-up position, which may be demonstrated via use of formal titles indicative of superior education, use of our last name while using their first name, or other indicators of presumed status and one-up-manship, we will not be very good at determining our client's level of assertiveness. We have to understand ourselves and our level of assertiveness in order to accurately gauge the other's interactive style. Hopefully, our own placement on the assertiveness continuum is within the healthier middle range so that we can more accurately distinguish whether our clients are highly assertive versus aggressive, in the middle, or less assertive versus passive in their interpersonal style.

If we, as therapists, accurately present ourselves somewhere within the middle range of healthy assertiveness, then how our clients present themselves to us will give us good information and clues about how they deal with others who are also within that range. If clients are overly aggressive with us or overly passive, that information will help us to assess how they generally deal with others. We become the assessment instrument, which requires ongoing monitoring for accuracy.

The second level of information comes from how clients describe their interpersonal relating with others in their lives. Ask clients questions about how they deal with people in authority, with their parents, bosses, and so on. Also ask them how they deal with people who are younger, who have less authority than they do, with employees, and with peers. The answers will provide you with valuable information about how clients see themselves in relationship to others: above, below, or beside.

Individuals can be passive, assertive, or aggressive. This dimension of an individual's interpersonal functioning can be fluid or fixed. If fluid, then the individual is able to be passive or assertive as the situation warrants. It is even healthy to be aggressive at times, as when one is under severe attack and there is no other viable option. If a person's interpersonal functioning is fixed, this means that the individual responds exactly the same way no matter what the interpersonal situation calls for. That is generally considered to be an unhealthy style of relating. Knowing when to be quiet, even though one is assertive, is considered to be an aspect of both maturity and wisdom. Speaking up, then, is measured in the context of the interpersonal relationship and the situation.

Accurately assessing an individual's position on the assertiveness continuum will provide the information necessary to the development of a good treatment plan.

TREATMENT PLANS: KNOWING HOW TO SPEAK, SPEAKING MORE, SPEAKING LESS

Assessment naturally leads to treatment planning. The treatment plan is a delineation of the goals for an individual based on assessed current functioning and desired outcomes. There are three types of goals that will likely be established for the skill of speaking up: To help an individual learn how to speak up, to help an individual speak up less, and to help an individual speak up more.

Relatively assertive people are not likely to show up as clients in our offices. If they do, treatment planning involves listening to what they say their needs are, helping them understand possible barriers to achieving their goals, and helping them develop specific plans whereby they can meet their needs. These treatment plans will often be focused on helping them listen or cooperate more effectively. Generally, these individuals will not need the help of a therapist for very long because they will address their issues directly with the people in their lives from whom they desire something. Individuals with excellent assertiveness skills do not generally need intervention in learning to speak up. They may need to tweak their speaking up skills to become even more effective.

Individuals with poor assertiveness skills definitely need to develop speaking up skills and can learn to do so via a focused treatment plan. Individuals who are moderately or highly assertive are not as likely to require psychological treatment, in general, as people who exhibit low assertiveness or who are passive. People with moderate assertiveness skills who believe that they require services will likely make their needs known (because they are assertive) and will, thereby, give themselves a better chance of getting what they need. Truly assertive people often get what they want, in part because they state what they want, listen to others, and are willing and able to negotiate for a deal that works for everyone involved, including themselves. The Family Wellness model refers to this type of negotiation as cooperation.

Learning How to Speak Up

Some people do not know how to speak up. They may have never been allowed to speak up for themselves as children, or they may have never seen it modeled within the family, or they may have never learned the ability to speak up. Other individuals speak up but do not communicate their needs effectively.

Individuals who do not know how to speak up may need basic instruction in communication strategies. Such individuals can learn to speak up by using the word "I" to start many sentences. They may need assurance that to do so is not being selfish or egocentric. They may need to learn that starting sentences with the words "You" or "Why" will likely result in the other person becoming defensive. These individuals may need to clearly know what they want and learn how to say so as specifically as possible to give themselves the best chance of getting what they want.

Individuals who are moderately to somewhat assertive may come to therapy when their needs are not being met in certain areas or with specific individuals who are important in their lives. In these situations, for example, within a marriage, significant friendship, at work, or with family members, individuals may speak up in an attempt to get their needs met. They recognize that they have a right to be heard and to get their needs met at least some of the time. If they are not successful in getting their needs met, they may try again a few times. After repeated unsuccessful efforts, these individuals will likely seek outside help. In the end, they may or may not get what they want. At the very least, however, they can have an assurance that they did everything possible to obtain what they seek. Assertiveness does not guarantee success. It guarantees that people give themselves the best chance of getting what they want.

Treatment plans for learning how to speak up, if properly constructed, can be highly productive. Focus on what clients are already doing well. Reinforcing pro-social behaviors will result in increased use of skills they already possess. All clients already have some speaking up or assertiveness skills. They likely have good listening skills. In fact, they may defer to others' needs a bit too much. Nevertheless, they are likely to have empathic responses upon hearing what other people need. In other words, they already have some of the basic skills. They simply need to practice a clearer expression of their needs, be more consistent in requiring consideration from others in their lives, and develop cooperation skills that take their own needs into account as much as the needs of others. Treatment plans may include specific ideas, such as the use of "I" statements, making needs known in specific and clear ways, and developing listening or cooperation skills.

Learning to Speak Up Less

Some individuals are so assertive that they go beyond the norm and become aggressive. These are the individuals identified by the Family Wellness model as bullies. Such individuals are not likely to show up in our offices unless they are referred for anger management or some similar issue, are being threatened with divorce, or are somehow identified as requiring help in their interpersonal relationships. Aggressive people are not likely to desire or seek treatment on their own because they believe that they are able to secure what they need. Their motto might be, "If you don't help yourself, nobody's going to do it for you." Or "God helps those who help themselves." These individuals may not seek treatment because they believe that a therapist cannot help by just talking. From their perspective, they may view conversation, which includes the ability to listen to other people and to their needs, as a sign of weakness. They will likely pride themselves on being self-made independent people, as rugged individualists. They view themselves as being strongly assertive, not aggressive.

These individuals know how to speak up. They need to learn how to speak up less. In other words, they need to learn how to listen more. Treatment plans for these individuals will highlight the concepts of empathy, taking turns speaking and listening, and looking for solutions that work for everyone involved, not just for the person speaking up.

If individuals who are bullies learn to listen more and slow down their natural inclination to speak up, they will likely find more cooperation from others and more successful interpersonal relationships. To be successful in working with these individuals requires the ability to answer the question, "What's in this for me?" Bullies have learned that they can get what they want by demanding it. What they have not learned is that they can have better, more affectionate, and more reciprocal interpersonal relationships by being willing to listen to others more while still asserting their needs.

Learning to Speak Up More

People who are extremely passive often will not get their needs met. They may become accustomed to being left out, isolated, and accommodating to the needs of others. They will come to treatment when they experience sufficient distress from their life predicament, when they learn that outside help is available, and when they develop some hope that the outside help may be useful. Often these clients may not easily recognize that their needs have gone unmet for a long time. Once they become aware of this reality, these clients may have difficulty in identifying specifically what they want.

Treatment planning with extremely passive individuals may be the most challenging of any type along the continuum of assertiveness. The therapist may want to do too much for, or on behalf of, these people. These clients may present as very distressed individuals who seem oppressed by life and by others in their lives. They may seem like lost souls. The therapist may want to rescue the hurting puppy. These clients may ask the therapist to do their work for them and the therapist may conspire with them to do their work. The manner of presentation may be, "Poor me. Help me." The therapist, if not careful, may be pulled in to help the individual in ways that only confirm the individual's perception of inadequacy. In such situations, the therapist could do more harm than good. The idea is to help individuals learn how to fish rather than giving them a fish.

For individuals who are highly passive, a starting point for treatment planning is to help them determine exactly what they want. Healthy assertiveness requires that individuals know what they want. In fact, the clearer individuals are about what they want, the better the chance of getting it.

To help individuals determine what they want, open-ended questions may be employed. As a therapist, it is important to listen and follow the client's lead. When clients are so passive that they don't know how to lead, the therapist may be tempted to take the lead. Bad idea. Listen, pause, and allow clients to suffer through some silence. In that process, they will likely begin to connect with their inner reality and to formulate what is desired. In this process, the therapist must be extremely patient.

> Zolton was in my office because he had never had a girlfriend and he wanted to ask a girl out on a date. The problem was that Zolton literally "froze" and was unable to speak in almost all interpersonal relationships, especially in the presence of women. Zolton would come into my office, say "Hello," and then sit in his chair for what seemed an eternity before making any other comment. I would attempt to ask open-ended questions in order to prompt him to express himself. The treatment plan for Zolton included a goal for me: Be quiet!

SPEAKING: TREATMENT PLANS

Through the development of a treatment plan, the therapist's task is to provide enough space for clients to help them determine what they want. Rather than continuing to push or to make suggestions about what clients may want, it is important to provide space for them. The clinician's silence will allow individuals to begin to think, without outside interference, about what they really want.

The therapist, at this point, listens intently and begins to help clients state what they want. Usually, people going through this agonizing process of trying to figure out what they want will finally say what they do not want (e.g., "I do not want to be told what to do," or "I do not want to wash the dishes"). In these situations, we help people go from negative (what they don't want) to positive (what they do want). For example, "I want to make my own decisions," or "I want to vacuum."

The next step is for the therapist to help individuals state what they want in a very specific fashion. Passive clients often will be very vague about what they want (e.g., "I want to be happier"). Individuals may need help to be specific about what they want (e.g., "I want to go out on a date every Thursday night"). Remember, communicating in a vague manner is likely a learned behavior. Individuals learn that they should not state what they want specifically due to likely negative outcomes, such as being disappointed, being rejected, or being attacked for saying what they want. The Family Wellness model teaches people to speak up very clearly and specifically for what they want and, at that point, not worry about the other's response. Some people have been taught that being extremely clear about what they want is selfish and egocentric. The therapist can teach passive individuals that speaking up for what they want is not only not selfish, it is actually one of the most selfless acts possible. Being assertive affirms not only ourselves but also the others around us. Stating our needs invites others to state their needs. In that process, agreements can be reached that hopefully will make life better for all involved.

Once individuals have determined what they actually want, in a very clear and specific manner (which is the first step in the development of a treatment plan for assertiveness), then they need to speak up for what they want. The treatment plan needs to include information about how, when, and with whom to speak up. These specifics will be developed by listening to clients about what needs are not being met and what they have decided that they want or need. Again, the more specific the treatment plan can be about what, how, when, and with whom, the better chance that individuals will actually accomplish the goals.

The generic treatment plan identifies the presenting or primary issue being addressed. In this chapter, we are concerned about helping people learn how to either speak up, speak up less, or speak up more. Therefore, the initial therapeutic task in the development of a treatment plan will be to listen to our client's hopes and dreams for the future that are affected by the ability to be assertive. After the desired outcome has been identified, then it must be determined who else will be involved in achieving it. Often the other people will include a spouse or significant other, a coworker, a boss, a relative, or a friend. Once those people have been identified, a variety of possible solutions can be explored, which will result in a list of potential interventions. The therapist can ask the client to pick one goal to implement. The implementation requires an answer to the following question: Who does what by when? In the case of assertiveness, the answer will almost always be that clients must take some speaking up actions with a person important in their lives. Finally, it must be decided how progress will be assessed. Figure 3.2 shows a sample completed treatment plan focused on assertiveness.

FIGURE 3.2
COMPLETED TREATMENT PLAN FOR ASSERTIVENESS

• Presenting or primary issue	*Unable to speak up for self.*
• Desired outcome	*I want a $3 per hour raise.*
• Who is needed to solve?	*Self, spouse, and boss.*
• Brainstorm solutions	*Quit and find another job.*
	Get a second job.
	Talk to boss about raise.
• Solution to implement	*I will ask boss for a raise*
• Who does what by when?	*This Wednesday, I will ask my boss for an appointment to talk about a raise. I will be clear and specific about what I want and why I deserve consideration for the raise. I will use "I" statements. I will be prepared to seek a second job if necessary.*
• Date to reevaluate progress	*I will speak with spouse about my decision and talk about family options. I will also meet with my therapist next Friday for scheduled appointment.*
• Alterations to plan	*None at this time. I will consider seeking a second job.*

Helping individuals learn how to be more assertive is not only helping them speak up; it is also helping them learn how to listen and how to co-operate to find solutions that work for all parties involved. However, the person who does not speak up likely already knows how to listen. In help-ing people to become more assertive, the focus is on speaking while not forgetting the importance of listening to others and caring about their needs.

When therapists help individuals develop their own treatment plans, they are more likely to pursue the plan and the results will be self-reinforcing, likely resulting in positive changes in their internal assessment of their capacity to function interpersonally.

Assertiveness training for people who are very passive is difficult. It can, however, be very satisfying to see individuals who have never spoken up for themselves learn and utilize skills in dealing with others. It can be equally gratifying to help individuals who have been bullies learn to listen, to make space for others, and to see the improved interpersonal results in their lives. Treatment plans can also be developed for individuals who are already relatively assertive and simply need some help in fine tuning their communication skills. In each of these three scenarios, the treatment plans (goals) will suggest practical interventions to effect change.

PRACTICAL INTERVENTIONS: THE ART OF SPEAKING UP WITHOUT BECOMING A BULLY

People who do not speak up often or well need practice. Interventions for assertiveness derive from a treatment plan that addresses the specific needs of the individual and that has been developed in conjunction with the client. Remember that treatment plans for assertiveness will likely focus on helping the individual learn how to speak up, to speak up less, or to speak up more.

How to Speak Up

In order to intervene appropriately, the mental health professional must make an accurate assessment of an individual's strengths and challenges. Make sure that the person is clear in specifying what he or she wants. The treatment plan will identify the client's goals for speaking up. A crucial part of the plan will be how the person will speak up, generally involving starting sentences with the word "I."

While using "I" to start sentences sounds like a gimmick or a simplistic communication technique, it is actually a very powerful weapon in the arsenal of an individual who is learning how to be assertive. Besides accepting responsibility for what follows in the sentence that starts with "I," the speaker begins to understand that he or she not only has needs but deserves to have those needs known and dealt with in any significant interpersonal relationships. It is a powerful way of communicating directly with others that does not bully. It is a means of inviting others into conversations. It is also a means of relieving internal pressures that develop when there are things that need to be said but are not expressed.

An amazing number of people do not know that it is acceptable to say things like, "I need . . .," or "I want . . .," or "I would appreciate . . ." Because these people have been taught that speaking up in this manner is selfish, aggressive, disrespectful, or in some other way inappropriate, many individuals do not have the skill of speaking up for what they want. These individuals need to give themselves permission to speak up assertively.

Regarding the acceptableness of speaking up without being de facto selfish, the therapist can play a game with the client, asking the client to determine the number between 1 and 100 that the therapist has chosen. After the client fails to divine the number, the therapist can discuss how few people really know how to read minds. "If your spouse, friend, coworker, or important other can read your mind, I guess you do not have to speak up with them. However, most people are not able to read minds. Therefore, practice makes better in terms of assertiveness." Also, clients can be reminded that if they constantly speak up and never listen or care about other people's needs, they are, in fact, selfish. Such is not normally the case for people who are seeking to learn how to speak up better.

When to Speak Up Less

Timing is everything in many aspects of life. This is especially true about knowing when to speak up. Just because we have something to say does not mean that it needs to be said immediately. The better part of valor is being able to sit with something if the timing is bad without sitting on it so long that the opportunity gets lost and the conversation never happens.

Some people speak up for what they want incessantly. They speak up so frequently that they have neither the time nor the inclination to listen to others. Such individuals have previously been described as bullies. There is a time to speak up and a time to listen. For clients in our office who have determined that their mouth gets them into a lot of trouble, practical interventions will seek to help them listen more to others. The clinician can ask such clients to carry 3 × 5 cards with them or have some other way of developing a baseline to document how often they speak up for their needs versus how frequently they listen to other people's needs. The goal for them is to increase the percentage of listening and reduce the percentage of speaking up.

Some individuals, not necessarily bullies, may have spoken up for their needs in the past but were punished in some way by others. Perhaps they were indelicate in their choice of when to speak up. Some people feel pressured to speak up, afraid that if they do not the moment will be lost and they will never get another opportunity to give voice to their needs. Others speak up when it is blatantly inappropriate because they do not know how to read social conversational cues.

When to Speak Up More

While silence may be golden at times, passive individuals need to speak up more frequently. Many individuals have suffered humiliation, rejection, or abandonment for speaking up. Over time, these individuals stopped believing that it was okay to speak up on behalf of their needs. They may have even lost hope that they could ever communicate effectively and get their needs met. Clearly, education about how and when to speak up is an important matter that can be dealt with in the therapy office.

The first important intervention is to ask people to clearly identify what they want to say. Talking out loud with the therapist can help them clarify what they want to say and give them practice in actually using words to express themselves. Clients can also be directed to write down what they want to say on a piece of paper, on the computer, or on some other device. Such expression of their thoughts and desires can help clients identify and clarify what they want by making them find words that match the desires of their hearts.

Ask clients who want to be more assertive to identify the best times and circumstances that will likely result in positive outcomes for a conversation. Examples for many people are after dinner, when rested, when calm, when sober, and so on. Being more assertive involves a willingness to speak up and knowing how to speak up, as well as knowing when to speak up. Some people are afraid to jump into a conversation for fear of interrupting and they let opportunities pass them by.

Besides deciding what to say and how and when to speak up, the treatment plan will identify with whom to speak. In other words, the message has to be delivered to the right person to be effective. From the treatment plan, clients may be asked to speak up to the therapist as a way of practicing speaking up to people in authority or, hopefully, to someone who is admired and respected. The therapist represents an excellent in vivo opportunity for clients to speak to because the therapist, by definition, will take a therapeutic stance (concern, acceptance, genuineness, and empathy; Yalom & Leszcz, 2005). The therapist cares for the well-being of clients, is nonjudgmental, is real with clients, and makes every effort to understand how difficult it is to become assertive for individuals who have spent most of their lives being passive. Ideally, clients will trust the therapist and the therapist will not disappoint. However, even if trust is not completely there, sometimes people are asked to "fake it 'til you make it." That is, practice speaking up even though it is difficult, and you may find that practice makes better. What was extremely difficult may become somewhat easier.

Besides speaking up with the therapist in the therapeutic setting, individuals should be afforded other opportunities for speaking up, for example, by asking clients to become involved with other people. Opportunities may be found in therapeutic social skills groups led by a therapist, or naturally occurring community-based groups (such as faith communities or service organizations). Group therapy is an ideal place where people can practice interpersonal dynamics. In that setting, individuals can learn from one another within the safety of a supportive environment. They can practice socialization skills, including the ability to speak up with others.

Ideally, once people have practiced speaking up within different treatment settings, they should be encouraged to generalize the learned skills with others important in their lives. This practice of assertiveness skills could involve friends and relatives as well as others in the community.

Because developing new assertiveness skills can be very difficult, mistakes will likely be made. The intervention plan must include opportunities for a feedback loop. When the person practices skills and succeeds, the success will likely result in a positive self-reinforcing feedback loop. Success breeds success. However, when someone is not successful, it is very important to have the opportunity to speak with the therapist to determine the specifics of what did not work and why. The person can then be instructed to return to the battle and engage in the new and desired behavior again. This process can be repeated as often as necessary until success is achieved. It is critical that interventions be small and specific enough to provide success experiences as often as possible.

Even after success occurs in the development of new assertiveness skills, additional practice is required to consolidate the gains achieved. During periods of stress, it is easy to revert to older, less effective means of interacting with others. With much practice in utilizing assertiveness techniques, the new skills can become old patterns. This new way of being can then become the new normal.

SUMMARY

People who are assertive, who speak up for themselves, can often be models for others to emulate. Some people may be so assertive that they actually become aggressive and need to learn to listen more. Others, who are mildly assertive, will at times get their needs met and will at other times accept not getting their needs met. They may subsume their desires to the needs of others as a conscious choice. They may speak up to a degree, but may choose not to continue seeking their needs and may be content with having only some of their needs met.

Satisfaction with the level of assertiveness achieved needs to be left in the hands of the client. It is the therapist's job to assess the client's stage of assertiveness at the initiation of treatment, to assist the client in determining what he or she wants to say, to provide skills for how to say it, and to help the client learn when to speak up and with whom to speak. The therapist can provide ongoing feedback to the client about progress toward assertiveness.

If treatment has gone well, the client will let the therapist know when the treatment goals have been achieved. Ultimately, the therapist should desire to be fired from the role of assertiveness instructor. If we do our job well, we will lose it. Well done.

4

Listen

Be a Follower

THE FAMILY WELLNESS model asserts that the ability to listen to others, and to care about what they are saying, is the second of three foundational skills necessary for an individual to be psychologically healthy. Listening is a gift. When we give it without any expectation of personal gain, it becomes the gift that keeps on giving.

The capacity to listen to another person is an important step in the development of intimacy in any relationship. When individuals habitually do not listen to others, they demonstrate that they are totally self-absorbed. They may have acquaintances, but they will likely not have friends. People who know how to listen likely know how to play well with others. Good listeners know how to be followers. They attend to the needs of others. Those actions are generally reciprocated and friendship has fertile ground in which to grow.

A conversation requires each person to know how to speak up as well as how to listen. Healthy interpersonal interaction requires the ability to listen to others. There is, however, a difference between listening and hearing. In Spanish, two totally separate words are used to differentiate between hearing and listening: *oír* and *escuchar*. The word *oír* refers to simply hearing sounds or spoken words. We may hear (*oír*) something or someone when conversation is not involved. For example, we may *oír* a door creaking or the words a person is saying without fully understanding the meaning behind the words or sounds. On the other hand, when we

104

listen to (*escuchar*) someone, we go beyond hearing to actually understanding the depth of the words' meaning, the feelings or intent of the message, and the energy level of the person speaking. To listen to another person is to make an important and intimate connection with that other person, even if we disagree with the other. To listen to someone does not mean that we necessarily agree with that person.

Most people want to be heard, to be understood, and to be agreed with. Good listeners seek to meet the first two expectations on that list. These two parts of listening are required in healthy interpersonal relationships. Complying with the third item is optional. Hearing someone denotes simply being aware of what the other person is saying. Being on the same page regarding the words exchanged is important in a conversation. Only hearing the words, however, is incomplete listening. To understand another means, "I get you." We hear the words and are aware of what they are saying at an emotional level. True listening requires that we attempt to achieve a deeper understanding of what the other person is saying at the word level, at the emotions level, and at the energy level. The words are the doorway to a person's thoughts. The feelings are the doorway to the emotions. The energy an individual exudes is the doorway to the person. When we truly listen to another, we are able to plumb the depths of who that person is, which is what intimacy is ("into-me-see"; see Figure 4.1).

People often get louder when they do not feel heard or understood. They presume that the other person must not have heard their words or

---

FIGURE 4.1
LEVELS OF LISTENING
(USED BY PERMISSION OF FAMILY WELLNESS ASSOCIATES)

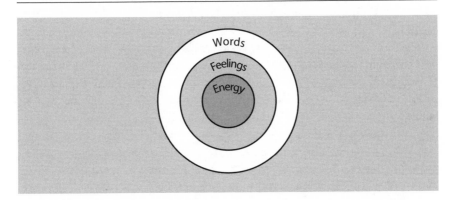

that they heard the words but did not understand them. The logic is that a higher volume will allow the other to both hear and understand. We know, unfortunately, that simply turning up the volume does not work. Think of a person speaking a foreign language that we do not understand. Will speaking louder allow us to understand the unknown language? No. After being unsuccessful at being heard and understood by being louder, individuals often shut down. Such a person goes inward, becomes quiet or sullen, and may even leave, either emotionally or physically. Therefore, many households are either very loud or very quiet. These conditions often are demonstrations of poor communication skills within the family.

Books on communication theory describe the multitude of barriers to effective communication, the reasons that make it difficult to actually listen to another. For example, as another person speaks, we are preoccupied with ourselves or distracted, and we are not fully present to attend to the other. Also, we have consciously or subconsciously established filters that prescribe to whom we are willing to listen, what we are willing to listen to, and when we will listen. These spam filters keep certain people and topics in or out. This reality is reflected in, for example, our proclivity to watch certain news broadcasts, which almost always precludes watching other news outlets. Our personal and familial histories tell us much about how we learned to listen (or not), what we are willing to listen to, to whom we are willing to listen, and the volume level that is required for us to actually listen to someone else.

The Family Wellness model proposes that healthy interpersonal relationships require a willingness to listen to others. This willingness is often based, in part, on the nature of the relationship previously established. People listen better when the other person speaks in a manner that is easy for us to accept. Most people are able to listen more easily to someone who starts sentences with the word "I" instead of "You" or "Why." Questions and "You" statements tend to push people away. "I" statements invite people into a conversation. It is easier to hear someone else when we do not feel that we have to defend ourselves.

Many filters get established in our formative years, on the listening side, that become barriers to effective communication over time. For example, if the volume was extremely loud at home in our family of origin, we either do not attend to someone who is speaking quietly or we may tune out someone who is speaking loudly. Before speaking, filters get established based on the speaker's sense of self, ability to trust, and willingness to accept risk, as well as the actual or perceived power differential between the parties in the conversation. With so many barriers and filters between speaker and listener, it is a wonder that any communication ever occurs.

We sometimes hear the words, "I'm not following you." That phrase has several possible meanings. It may mean that the speaker is not being clear in pursuing some logical sequence or is not using words that are understandable to the speaker. It may also mean that the listener is preoccupied with other things and is not focusing on the speaker's message. Or other barriers may exist on the listener's or speaker's side to prevent the completion of the communication loop. It may also mean that the listener does not care to put sufficient energy into what is being said to truly hear what the person is attempting to communicate.

That last possibility, in part, relates to a person's capacity for empathy. When we care about another person's perspective and are willing to listen to that person (whether we agree with him or not), we demonstrate the capacity for empathy. Empathy has been described as being able to put ourselves in the shoes or moccasins of others. Another definition of empathy is the capacity to accurately discern the words, the feelings, and the energy that the other person is expressing. When we understand another person, we are hearing the words and plumbing deeper levels of the other person's emotions and intensity of energy. When we understand another person in that way, we really know the other as an individual.

The Family Wellness model proposes that a listener has choices. We come to a fork in the road and have to decide which direction we will follow. We can choose to look for connection, for respect, and for understanding. Or we can choose to focus on problems, arguments, reactions, and fights. Healthy listening requires that individuals have a good sense of self and a desire to connect with others, otherwise known as the two jobs of every individual. Without these strengths, an individual will be unable to establish a healthy dyadic relationship. Healthy listening also demands that we know both how to listen and how much to listen. Too much listening will result in our needs being trampled while too little listening will prevent true connection. There is an art to being a good listener without becoming a wimp.

ASSESSMENT: LISTENING FOR HOW WELL A PERSON LISTENS

The Family Wellness model asserts that the ability to listen to others is an indicator of an individual's capacity for intimacy. People who listen find value in others and know how to connect with them. It is presumed that an individual who can listen well is more empathic than one who is not a good listener. Sometimes difficulties in social interactions occur because of deficits in the skill of listening. Before treatment plans can be developed to determine the best interventions, an assessment of listening is required.

The assessment of listening is more difficult than the assessment of speaking up. To assess speaking up, clinicians can listen to clients' words for frequency, tone, level, and directness. To assess the ability to listen, clinicians must discern between quiet that demonstrates true listening and quiet that shows a variety of other potential realities: boredom, disinterest, lack of understanding, lack of caring, and so on. Mental health professionals need to assess an individual's level of listening by attending to the continuum of listening, which extends from not knowing how to listen to listening too much or too little.

The therapist will determine a client's placement along the continuum of listening by observing several indicators of effective listening, which include the ability to be quiet and the ability to reflect what is being heard at the word, emotion, and energy levels, and by paying attention to behavioral cues that demonstrate either good or poor listening.

An individual who is good at listening knows how to be quiet. It is hard to hear when our mouths are open. When our clients demonstrate that they cannot keep from speaking, they likely either do not know how to listen or listen too little. Silence is a good place to start in assessing this skill.

Some people speak before a question or comment by the other person has been completed. These individuals may be quick thinkers who are several steps ahead of the conversation. They may enjoy quick repartee. They may be good listeners, but the chances are that they are so invested in what they have to say that they do not take the time necessary to actually listen to others. They are more interested in talking than in listening. They may also have attention deficits or difficulties with impulsivity.

Other people are willing to let someone drone on and on for an extremely long time before they interject any opinions, elicit information, or ask clarifying questions. These individuals may not speak up enough to be effective, active listeners.

Therapists know that being an excellent listener is not just about being quiet. We know that being a good listener means reflecting back to the speaker what one has heard, how one understands the emotions of the other, and the energy level that is being projected by the speaker. That is what is known as active listening. How well an individual actively listens to others is one way of assessing placement of that individual on a continuum.

The third area the therapist must explore when assessing an individual's ability to listen is behavioral manifestations, which generally include appropriate levels of eye contact, being quiet, making brief sounds intended to show understanding, nods, repeating a few words or feelings, matching the energy of the speaker, summarizing, and pacing the dialogue (the ability to wait until the speaker is done). Conversely, other verbal and behavioral manifestations of poor listening include interruptions, judgments, criticisms, and questions.

In effective listening, there is a very important balance between knowing how to listen, taking time to listen, and being willing to give an observation or opinion to make the conversation an actual dialogue instead of a monologue. The assessment of listening requires that the therapist be an excellent listener. The clinician listens to the words being said, the quiet being preserved, the reflection of words, feelings, energy, and the behavioral cues that demonstrate excellent listening.

The clinician sometimes has only one source of information to determine whether someone is a good listener. The client may be in a dyadic relationship with the therapist: only the two of them are in the room. In such situations, the therapist must first listen for how well the client is listening in the three arenas noted above (the ability to be quiet, the ability to reflect, and the behavioral cues for listening). Second, the therapist must be able to provide the client with opinions regarding the client's ability to listen. Third, the clinician must assess how well the client hears what is being said. It is through this feedback loop that the clinician will ascertain whether the initial assessment was correct or not. If the client corrects the therapist's judgments, then the clinician must determine if those comments represent appropriate corrective feedback or if the client is unable to hear the clinician's opinions and is minimizing, rationalizing, or externalizing and, therefore, not listening well.

More often, the clinician is in the therapy room with a couple or a family. In these situations, the therapist is in a wonderful position to see how well people listen to one another. The therapist can either prompt the people in the room to talk with one another on a difficult topic or simply assess how the people are interacting. Since people in group interactions tend to respond the way they usually do in real life, the clinician simply has to provide a safe place for people to interact. The clinician will soon see the skills of listening (or the lack of skills) enacted before his or her very eyes. The mental health professional can then hear and observe the three factors noted above and make a determination about a particular individual's ability to listen.

Naturally, to assess the skill of listening, the therapist must have good clinical skills, the ability to listen well, and the capacity to discern between silence that reflects good listening and silence that reveals a lack of listening. Clinicians need to assess their own ability to listen. If we listen too little, it will be hard to hear our clients as they express themselves and it will be hard for us to accurately read how well they are listening. Clinicians who listen too much will not be directive enough to quickly determine clients' capacity for listening. We may draw the assessment process out so far that we will be unable to read the verbal and nonverbal cues that demonstrate whether our clients have capacity and skills, or whether they listen too much or too little.

The therapist must also determine the individual's motivation for either listening or not listening. Some people who have excellent listening skills choose to not listen to certain individuals, to certain themes, or at specific times. These individuals know how to listen, but in given circumstances listen either too much or too little. The therapist must determine if an individual has skills or deficits, or why an individual listens too little or too much.

The assessment of the capacity to listen will drive the development of a treatment plan. Once the therapist has a good sense of the client's listening skills, then a plan will suggest itself that will allow for the development of specific treatment goals and improved potential for ultimate success in the therapy process.

TREATMENT PLANS: KNOWING HOW TO LISTEN, LISTENING LESS, LISTENING MORE

There are three types of goals that will likely be established for the skill of listening: helping an individual learn how to listen, to listen less, or to listen more.

Some individuals do not know how to listen and do not care. They will not likely be voluntarily seen in our offices. They may come in as court-ordered referrals or because an important person in their lives has threatened them if they do not seek outside help. These individuals will, by definition, not be particularly open to listening to what the therapist has to say. For them, the interactive strategies of the Family Wellness model can be particularly effective and necessary if they are going to benefit from psychotherapy. If these strategies are not utilized, the course of treatment will likely be short lived.

Some people listen well but do not know how to speak up. These individuals may need assistance in establishing boundaries with others. Because effective listeners tend to care for others, they may take on the burden of trying to fix the other person's issues. They may require assistance in recognizing that they cannot change someone else. They may need to enhance their speaking or cooperation skills to balance their listening skills. These people need to listen less.

Some people do not know how to listen and they are distressed because they experience interpersonal difficulties. These individuals need education regarding effective communication strategies. In particular, they will likely benefit from understanding the importance of listening to others and learning attitudinal and behavioral skills that will enhance their capacity to listen. These individuals are generally hungry to learn and will devour what the therapist has to offer. These individuals need to listen more.

Individuals who know how to listen to others well and are also able to set appropriate boundaries in their relationships will not likely show up as clients in our offices. If they do, treatment planning will generally involve helping them develop specific plans for speaking up or cooperating more effectively.

Learning How to Listen

Some people never learned to listen; they may have never seen it modeled within the family; or they may have been oblivious to the need for listening. For some, the egocentric developmental periods of infancy, toddlerhood, and even adolescence may have become entrenched as the modus operandi of living. Not listening may reflect a personality flaw (which in the extreme can be viewed as narcissism or some similar personality defect or mental illness) or may represent a lack of skills development. Although clarification of the etiology of this trait is important, it is not the most cogent part of developing a treatment plan. What is most important is what the client desires as an appropriate outcome for participation in treatment. If individuals simply want to show that they attended a course of counseling and want to be done, the prognosis for a successful outcome will be very guarded. If, on the other hand, individuals want to understand themselves more and hope for change in their functioning capacity, then the prognosis is significantly more hopeful.

> Jerry, his wife, and their teenage daughter and 10-year-old son came for an initial psychotherapy session. Jerry informed me that he was in my office under duress, that his wife had threatened to leave him if he did not do something about the lack of family connection. He started talking and gave the others little opportunity to interrupt him. He was clear with me that he did not believe in therapy, and that he believed it was a waste of time and money and for people who didn't know how to make decisions. Shortly after he made these disclosures, he left and took his family with him. I never saw them again. I still worry about those individuals.

Individuals who do not know how to listen and do not care will likely not participate in psychotherapy for very long. They will not see any value in the treatment and may not be open to any interventions. The therapist who simply listens (no matter how empathically) may not be useful in effecting change, since clients may eloquently and repeatedly express that they do not have a problem, that the problem is with the person who referred them to counseling, and that they wish to terminate treatment as soon as possible. The therapist who simply talks to the client (no matter how brilliantly) will definitely not be effective, as the client will not be listening anyway. Any chance of connecting with these individuals will be based on utilizing interactive strategies. However, the clinician first needs to elicit the individual's goals for participation in treatment.

Individuals who do not listen well may ask, "What's in it for me?" They tend to be self-focused and view the world in an egocentric manner for a variety of reasons. It is exactly this worldview that prevents them from having mutually satisfying interpersonal relationships and is precisely why they show up in the therapist's office, if they do. It is not that they do not have the capacity to care for others; it is that their own needs preempt the needs of others.

An individual who states something like "Other people think that I do not listen well" will also likely identify as a goal something like "I want them to know that I listen." The goal will need to be revised because it is an outcome for someone who is not in the treatment room. A better statement of the goal would be, "I want to behave in a way that lets others know that I am a good listener. I want to listen to what my spouse says."

Some individuals do not listen because they have a skills deficit. They may need basic instruction in communication strategies. They can learn to listen by utilizing certain strategies, such as learning to be quiet until another person has completed his thought or sentence. Then the listener can demonstrate listening by making appropriate eye contact and can reflect to the other person that he is listening by noticing the words being spoken, the emotions being expressed, and the energy level of the speaker. The listener can do all of this by beginning most sentences with the word "you." For example, "You're tired; you're sad; you're mad." When listeners start a reflective statement with "you," they are reminded to focus on the speaker. Listeners may need assurance that they will have a chance to express their own needs later. These newbie listeners need to learn how to share. Relationships work best when individuals take turns listening and speaking up.

Treatment plans for learning how to listen, if properly constructed, can be highly productive. Focus on what clients are already doing well. Reinforcing pro-social behaviors will result in increased use of skills they already possess. All clients already have some listening skills, even if they are not very effective listeners. These individuals will likely have good speaking up skills. They may need to enhance their listening skills to balance their already excellent speaking up skills. They may need to practice patience while others express their needs. They also have to refrain from attempting to solve other people's problems. To listen to another person does not necessarily mean that the other person wants the listener to solve the problem. Learning to balance listening with speaking can then lead to utilizing both individuals' cooperation skills for problem solving. Such an outcome can produce more mutually satisfying interpersonal relationships.

Learning to Listen Less

Some individuals demonstrate a very good skill—being a caring listener—and take it to an extreme. These individuals are identified by the Family Wellness model as wimps. Such individuals are very likely to show up in our offices only when their caring for others has become such a significant burden that they have lost themselves in the process.

These individuals always listen to others. Yet when they have a need to talk, they are seldom able to find anyone who will listen to them. These individuals engage in one-way relationships that are other-focused. If this situation continues for a long time, individuals will become tired, angry, and resentful but will continue the same habits. They define themselves as caring individuals. It is a very good thing to listen and to care for others. These individuals, however, have lost themselves and tend to be very unhappy, predominantly because their needs are not being met and because their relationships are unidirectional and unsatisfying.

These people need to speak up more and set appropriate boundaries. They need to learn how to listen less. Treatment plans for these individuals will highlight the concepts of self-care, taking turns speaking and listening, and looking for solutions that work for everyone involved, not just for the person speaking.

Some people believe that it is selfish to speak up, so they learn to listen, to a fault. If they ever do speak up for their needs and deny another person's requests for time and attention, they may be told that they are being selfish. In those situations, I ask them to say (at least, to themselves), "Thank you for noticing. I am taking better care of myself!"

If wimps learn to speak up more and manage their natural inclination to care for others, they will likely find more satisfying and successful interpersonal relationships. To be successful in working with these individuals requires the ability to help them understand that taking good care of ourselves is necessary so that we have more to give to others. In that sense, to provide self-care is one of the most unselfish things we can do in our human relationships.

Learning to Listen More

We know that some people do not listen to others and do not care. Others do not listen well yet desire to learn to do so. We know that people who do not listen to others will often find themselves in difficult interpersonal dynamics. They will be viewed as self-centered and will be shunned by others or will be tolerated but will have only very superficial relationships. The best argument for listening more and caring for what others are saying is the potential for increased intimate connection.

Most individuals who do not play well with others because they fail to listen will not get their deepest needs met. They may get what they externally desire because they are good at speaking up for themselves, but their more basic need for connection may go unsatisfied. They often come to treatment when they experience sufficient distress from their life predicament, when they learn that outside help is available, and when they develop sufficient hope that the outside assistance may be useful.

Treatment planning with individuals who do not listen is challenging.

The clinician must determine what the client desires as an outcome. People who do not listen well may not have the best empathy to be able to understand why the others in their life are so frustrated with them. Therefore, sufficient time has to be spent in listening to clients to ascertain specifically what they want and what they need to become more effective listeners.

It is not easy to identify exactly what is happening internally when a person is silent. When an individual does not speak up well, the clinician can either tune into the silence or can help shape the message being conveyed.

If an individual consistently speaks up while someone else is still talking, the individual needs to be quiet longer. If, however, the person is quiet, who can tell if the person is listening? When someone is silent, it is more difficult to divine his or her internal process. Fortunately, when a client does not listen much, it is likely that the individual is good at speaking up. In that case, the therapist must use listening skills to understand what happens internally with the client that interferes with good listening. Then those factors can be developed into specific, measurable, attainable, reasonable, and time-limited goals.

Listening: Treatment Plans

The clearer we are about what we want, the better the chance of getting it. To help individuals determine what they want in terms of listening more, open-ended questions may be employed. As a therapist, it is important to listen and follow the client's lead in the development of treatment goals.

People going through the process of figuring out what they want will often say what they do not want (e.g., "I do not want to talk about myself when someone is speaking"). In those situations, we help the person go from negative (what they don't want) to positive (what they do want). For example, "I want to be a better friend by listening more to my friend's words, feelings, and energy." Therapists often need to help clients state what they want in a very specific fashion.

The Family Wellness model teaches people to listen to other people's words, which are the doorway to their thoughts; to their feelings, which are the doorway to the emotions; and to their energy, which is the doorway to the person. To be an effective listener means that we have to put our needs (or our agenda) aside for awhile. There are many reasons why people hesitate to lay aside a discussion of their needs. For one, some people fear that if they do not speak up for their needs now, the moment will pass and their needs will never be met. Such an individual needs to develop an appreciation for delayed gratification. Other people worry that if they do not speak about their needs immediately, the other person will develop a sense of entitlement and the dynamic between the individuals may become unbalanced. To fully listen to someone else requires that we have patience both with ourselves and with the other person. We must attend to the person, put our needs off for awhile, and be fully present for the other person. We must also learn to trust the process. It is like a teeter-totter. Both people need to speak, but not at the same time. Both people need to listen, but not at the same time. Learning to become comfortable with being silent is an important component in our ability to listen more. If we listen now, there will be a chance to speak up later. That pattern is what makes a conversation mutually satisfying.

Once individuals have learned what they want in terms of listening better, in a very clear and specific manner (which is the first step in the development of a treatment plan), then they need to practice that behavior. The treatment plan needs to include information about how, when, and with whom to listen. These specifics will be developed by listening to clients speak about what happens when they are ineffective at listening. The more specific the treatment plan can be about what, how, when, and with whom, the better the chance that the individual will actually accomplish the goals.

The generic treatment plan identifies the presenting or primary issue. In this chapter, we are concerned about helping people learn how to listen, listen less, or listen more. The initial therapeutic task in developing a treatment plan is to listen to our client's hopes and dreams for the future that are affected by the inability to listen well. After the desired outcome has been stated, then all individuals involved in achieving the desired outcome must be identified. Often the others will include a spouse or significant other, a coworker, a boss, a relative, or a friend. Once those people have been identified, a variety of possible solutions can be explored. This process is often referred to as brainstorming. The possible solutions will result in a list of potential interventions, one of which can be chosen by the client. Implementation requires an answer to the question: Who does what by when? In this case, the answer will almost always be that the client must take some listening action with a person important in his or her life. Finally, the question of how progress will be assessed must be answered.

FIGURE 4.2
COMPLETED TREATMENT PLAN FOR LISTENING

• Presenting or primary issue	*Spouse thinks I do not listen well.*
• Desired outcome	*I want to let my spouse know that I hear and understand, even when I do not agree.*
• Who is needed to solve?	*Self and spouse only.*
• Brainstorm solutions	*Argue my point.* *Cave in to spouse's requests.* *Tell spouse the words I hear and the emotions I think are being expressed.*
• Solution to implement	*Tell spouse the words I hear and the emotions I think are being expressed.*
• Who does what by when?	*Tonight, I will ask my spouse for 30 minutes to talk about each of our hopes and dreams for the future. I will listen carefully to my wife. I will reflect some of the words I hear her say and take guesses at what the emotions are behind her words. I will wait until my spouse is finished speaking without interrupting. I will use "you" statements.*
• Date to reevaluate progress	*I will speak with spouse about our visions for the future next Wednesday evening and will schedule a date night to continue our discussions about each of our hopes and dreams for the future.*
• Alterations to plan	*None at this time. I will seek to listen more carefully to her emotions and not only to her words in the future. I will request feedback from her about whether she feels heard and understood by me.*

Figure 4.2 shows a sample completed treatment plan focused on listening.

Helping individuals learn how to be better listeners is not only about encouraging them to be quiet. It is also about being focused and attentive to the words, the emotions, and the energy level of the other person.

Good listening is putting aside other distracters, such as cell phones, television, and whatever else prevents us from fully attending to what another person is saying.

Some people need skills for listening. Those skills can be taught. What cannot be taught is care and concern for another. Other people need to listen less by becoming more assertive and establishing appropriate boundaries. These people already care for others but do so at the expense of their own needs. Yet others need to listen more despite knowing what good listening entails. These individuals are already good at speaking up for their own needs but must learn to put their needs aside for awhile in order to attend to the needs of others. In each of these three scenarios, individuals benefit from improved interpersonal relationships based on more effective listening.

When therapists help individuals develop their own treatment plans, clients are more likely to pursue their goals and the results will be self-reinforcing. Improved listening almost always leads to increased intimacy. Specific treatment plans suggest the practical interventions required to make the goals reality in the lives of our clients.

PRACTICAL INTERVENTIONS: THE ART OF LISTENING WITHOUT BECOMING A WIMP

People who do not listen often or well need practice. Interventions for the development of listening skills derive from a treatment plan that addresses the specific needs of the individual and that has been developed in conjunction with the client. Treatment plans will likely focus on helping the individual learn how to listen, listen less, or listen more.

How to Listen

The mental health professional must make an accurate assessment of the client's strengths and challenges in order to develop a treatment plan that will provide for practical, effective interventions. It is not enough to determine that a problem exists; it is necessary to determine the desired outcome to give clients the best chance of getting what they want. The treatment plan will identify the client's goals for listening. A crucial part of the plan will be how the person will listen, generally involving being quiet at first, reflecting words, emotions, and feelings, and starting most reflective statements with the word "you."

While using "you" to start sentences sounds like a simplistic gimmick, it is actually a very important means of helping an individual become a better listener. Starting with "you" reflects the assumption that when listening it is important to focus on the other and not on the self. This focus on the other is why listening is considered to be a gift that we give to another person.

For people who do not know how to listen, the clinician must intervene at a very basic level. Although most people acknowledge that being quiet when someone else is speaking is the essence of listening (besides being polite), it is amazing how many people are not quiet when another is attempting to communicate with them. People often ask questions, direct the focus of attention back to themselves, or otherwise interrupt the speaker. The therapist can ask clients to practice being quiet for a longer period than they normally do when they are making efforts at listening. It is important to teach clients to refrain from asking questions unless they are for clarification, to withhold judgment until they have heard the entire story, and to reflect the speaker's words, emotions, and energy.

The Family Wellness clinician will often have a mirror handy to demonstrate that when we listen to another we are acting as a mirror. As we reflect the words, the speaker knows that we are hearing. As we guess at the feelings, the speaker knows that we understand. And as we reflect the speaker's energy level, the speaker correctly believes that the listener not only hears the words and understands the message, but comprehends the messenger.

Although the clinician can refer clients to books or classes on communication, the best intervention is available in the therapy room with whatever number of people are present. If only the client and therapist are in the room, the therapist can give the client a certain number of fuzzy balls (or similar objects). The therapist will then ask the client to listen to the therapist on a topic that might be difficult for the client to hear. As the client asks questions, changes the subject, or otherwise interrupts and shows poor listening, the therapist will remove the fuzzy balls one by one. Subsequently, the therapist can remind the client of the attitudinal, verbal, and behavioral skills involved in effective listening. They can then repeat the previous conversation, except that the therapist will hold the objects and give them to the client one by one as the client displays effective listening skills. This activity can be not only fun but very instructive.

If a couple or various family members are present with the therapist, the conversation can be among the others in the room with the therapist monitoring the skills being practiced by the listener. The topics discussed can be some predetermined hot topic such as politics or religion, or can be based on what the therapist knows is particularly difficult for the client to discuss.

When to Listen Less

Some people are such good listeners that they never speak up. The Family Wellness model refers to them as wimps. There is definitely a time to listen and a time to speak up. We may choose to continue listening at times because we believe that others need to talk, to vent, or to otherwise continue to express themselves. However, if we notice that in a particular dyadic relationship we are always the one listening and the other is always the one speaking, we have identified an imbalance that needs to be corrected in order for the relationship to be mutually satisfying and for true intimacy to develop.

Problems in relationship often occur because of power differentials in the two complementary skills of speaking and listening. For example, take the case of Andrea and Aaron.

> From the moment they met, Andrea knew that Aaron was exactly the man she should spend the rest of her life with. He was right in so many different ways. His most lovable quality was the way that he seemed not only to know what she wanted but also what she needed. Aaron sometimes knew what Andrea wanted before Andrea knew. Also, he certainly knew what he wanted. Aaron had no problem speaking up for what he wanted, whether it was about what to have for dinner, what type of clothes looked good on Andrea, or a myriad of other insights about what she needed. With his intellect, insight, and decision-making qualities, Andrea was sure that not only would Aaron be successful in his future but that they would go far together.

As so often happens in romantic relationships, the leader was looking for a follower and the follower was looking for a leader. A match made in heaven—at first. Over time, Andrea began to realize that she had no voice in the relationship. She had been so awestruck by Aaron that she listened to him unreservedly. She felt she could learn so much from him that she forgot herself in the relationship equation. She listened so much and spoke so little that, eventually, she lost herself. She went from being a good listener to being a wimp in that particular relationship.

Although listening is an excellent skill and caring for others is an admirable quality, it is important to appreciate that there is a time to listen and a time to speak. Finding balance in utilizing these two complementary skills is what allows people to appreciate their individuality and also allows the forging of healthy connections with others.

For clients who have realized that they listen much more than they speak in certain relationships, practical interventions will help them practice listening less and speaking up more. The clinician can ask clients to carry 3 × 5 cards with them or have some other way of developing a baseline to document how often they listen to others versus how frequently they express their own needs. The goal is to increase the percentage of speaking and reduce the percentage of listening.

Some individuals, not necessarily wimps, may listen to others out of a caring heart but find it difficult to express their needs. These individuals need to value themselves not only for the gift they can give others via listening but also for the gift of simply being who they are. The gift of listening can become unappreciated, taken for granted, and presumed as an entitlement if it is not balanced with the gift of speaking up for what we need.

When to Listen More

Some people know how to listen, but are not frequently inclined to do so. This strident failure to listen often results in a lack of intimate connections. These individuals may care for others and have empathy. However, they so infrequently demonstrate that care that others distance themselves. This emotional distance may increase over time until people who were previously friends may become strangers, and people who were previously intimate may simply become roommates. It is the breaking of important relationships or the cooling of these connections that drive some people to seek professional help.

Some people may lose hope that they can ever learn to listen to another person. Education about how and when to listen are important matters that can be dealt with in the therapy office.

Marvin came to the therapist's office because his wife threatened to leave him if he did not. His wife did not feel that Marvin was capable of under- standing her. He never seemed to listen and did not demonstrate any effort at caring about her life or situation. After several therapy sessions where interpretations were made about his wife's underlying feelings and overall emotional state, Marvin wondered out loud, "Am I from Mars? Why don't I understand my wife? I just don't!"

The first important intervention in getting people like Marvin to become better at listening is to get them to commit to becoming heroic listeners. Clients can be asked to write out a job description that specifies the differ- ent attitudinal and behavioral factors that are important components of listening. They can then be asked to sign a contract, a commitment, to being that type of listener. Finally, they can be asked to submit reports of examples of heroic listening that they either participated in with others, that they observed between others, or that they saw on television during the period between appointments. These summaries will reinforce the in- dividual's commitment to observing and implementing the different as- pects of effective listening. Clients need to see progress in themselves in order to develop hope that change is possible. The therapist is in an excel- lent position to reinforce what the client has done well. While we ac- knowledge that the individual may not have done everything well, the Family Wellness clinician chooses to focus on what the client did well. That reinforcement produces a positive feedback loop that turns into an upward spiral that produces more active listening skills.

Treatment plans need to identify situations in which the client will lis- ten more to others, how to listen to others, in what circumstances, and to whom the individual will listen. Clients are encouraged to become in- volved with other people through participation in therapeutic social skills groups led by therapists, or naturally occurring community-based groups (such as faith communities or service organizations). Since listening leads to greater intimacy, fears regarding increased connection can be addressed in the therapy setting.

Even after listening skills improve, additional practice is required to consolidate the gains achieved. Under stress, it is easy to revert to older, less effective means of interacting with others. Listening well often leads to increased intimacy, which can be difficult for some people. Care should be taken to provide people who are new to listening with sufficient sup- port to help them deal with the increased depth of interaction with others.

A balanced approach to listening becomes a gift to others as well as to ourselves.

SUMMARY

Silence is golden. Listening includes silence and it also requires active investment in what the other person is saying and who the other person is. Listening is a gift. Listening does not require agreement. Listening requires respect.

Some people may be so good at listening that they actually become passive and need to learn to speak up more. Others may need to learn and practice the actual nuts and bolts of listening: being quiet and reflecting words, emotions, and energy. They may need to develop the attitudinal and behavioral skills of listening. Some will know how to listen but may need to modulate it, listening either more or less.

Satisfaction with the level of listening needs to be left in the hands of the client. The client is the expert on his life. It is the therapist's job to assess the client's skill level at the initiation of treatment, to assist the client in determining what outcome is desired, and to provide a safe place to practice the skill as well as providing ideas for when, where, and with whom the client can practice the skill of listening. The therapist can provide ongoing feedback about progress toward these goals.

5

Cooperate

Negotiating for Solutions That Work

MOVING PARTS IN close proximity create friction. That friction can severely damage machinery. Likewise, people sometimes damage their relationships because of the intensity of their differing hopes and dreams.
People need to work together to find solutions to their differences. Since
no man or woman is an island, the Family Wellness model believes that
everyone needs to demonstrate the three core skills: speak, listen, and cooperate. Cooperation is the grease that lubricates relationships, thereby
either preventing or repairing damage. Cooperation is the skill that promotes harmony within relationships.

Cooperation is the utilization of speaking and listening skills in the service of finding solutions that work for all parties involved. Cooperation is
finding a balance between one's needs and the needs of others. Cooperation means, "I want a good deal for me and I want a good deal for you."
Occasionally, cooperation is coming to the conclusion that the best we
can do is to agree to disagree. The ability to work toward a solution that
works for everyone requires an investment in the word "We."

Rebecca was a young woman who desperately wanted to be liked and was
very giving. She had roommates that took advantage of her kindness and
who did not pay their rent on time, if at all. She had boyfriends that demanded much but offered little in return. Others in her life believed in the
principle of give and take—she was supposed to give and they would take.
Finally, as a result of professional counseling, Rebecca realized that these

other people in her life were not true friends. They hung around only because of what she had to offer. She put her foot down and started saying what she wanted. Rebecca would agree to what others wanted only if she decided that it was good for her to do so. She learned how to say no. She clearly declared what she needed in her relationships. In that process, some of the others faded into history, called her selfish, or otherwise stopped engaging with her. Rebecca was sad to see some of these people go, but came to realize that friendship and intimacy can only be achieved in a world where people give and receive in a reciprocal manner. She also realized that what she did had an impact on how others responded to her.

People often think of cooperation as the ability to compromise. Some marriage researchers opine that compromise is the optimal skill in maintaining long-term relationships. The Family Wellness model disagrees. Compromise may mean that, after some negotiation, I get some of what I want and the other person gets some of what he or she wants; however, neither of us gets what we really want. If I want Chinese food and the other person wants Italian food, we may compromise and go to a Mexican restaurant. While that compromise meets some of our needs (eating and spending time together), neither of us gets what we really want in terms of cuisine. Cooperation is the idea that each of us can get what we want, although not necessarily immediately or at the same time. A negotiated settlement using cooperation skills may mean that we go to an Italian restaurant tonight and the next time we will go to a Chinese restaurant. Another solution might be to go the food court at the mall where they have both Chinese and Italian food. Occasionally, we may need to compromise. More often, however, we should seek to cooperate. Cooperation works toward a win-win instead of a lose-lose.

Since cooperation means, in part, that I want a good deal for me, I need to know what I want. As I come to understand exactly what I want, I will be able to clearly say what I want. After I state what I want, I need to wait and listen to what the other person has to say. Incidentally, I also have to care about what he or she wants (especially if I want a reciprocal, egalitarian relationship). I neither have to agree with what the other person says nor do I have to comply with his or her requests or demands. I do need to carefully listen to the other's words, feelings, and energy. Since cooperation also means that I want a good deal for the other person, I have to listen to what that person wants. By spending enough time listening and looking for common ground, I give myself the best chance of continuing a dialogue and negotiating toward a solution that may work for both parties. When individuals fail to state a position precisely or fail to listen adequately, they will likely experience frustration, or some other dissatisfaction, with the results of a conversation and a relationship. In some cases, continued failure to communicate reveals a failure to connect on the part of one or both individuals. In those cases, the individuals involved will either stop being in any type of relationship or will develop an unhealthy dynamic within the relationship.

Another aspect of cooperation involves the power differential between the individuals in a system. Some relationships are, by definition, unequal, such as parents and their children. Parents are leaders and models. Parents are supposed to make rules, stick together, and stay in charge. Parents make rules and children are supposed to follow them. Even when parents are models for their children (making time to play, listen, encourage, and talk together), the adults deliberately and temporarily suspend their authority as leaders in order to connect with their children. The worth and value of parents and children are the same but the roles are different. Parents are in charge; kids are not. Ditto for the relationship between bosses and employees, teachers and students, and guards and prisoners. Other relationships are purposefully egalitarian. Many people believe that spousal relationships ought to be coequal. If a couple does not want their relationship to be coequal, they can cooperatively define how their relationship will be structured. Other coequal relationship categories include coworkers, siblings, and members of a team.

In relationships that are purposefully or actually unequal, the listening skill is particularly important for the one-down person. Even in this type of relationship, there will be times when the individual in the lower role needs to speak up. How the individual speaks up will make all the difference in terms of achieving a successful solution when problems develop. Ideally, the person in the position of authority (who generally already knows how to speak up) will also be a good listener. Being respectful by listening to subordinates promotes healthier dynamics. In relationships which are coequal, both speaking and listening skills need to be used in balance to achieve solutions that work for all the parties involved.

Often, individuals are not able to cooperate well because they do not know how to speak up, when to speak, when to listen, or how much to cooperate or negotiate in a given situation. It is critical for all individuals to know how to cooperate, how much to speak, and how much to listen. An assessment of whether an individual knows how to cooperate and how well the individual balances the skills of speaking, listening, and cooperating will lead the clinician toward effective treatment planning and practical interventions.

ASSESSMENT: THE TEETER-TOTTER TEST— ARE WE HAVING FUN YET?

The Family Wellness model posits that the ability to cooperate reveals an individual's capacity for connection. Cooperation is an indicator of whether an individual plays well with others. If the most important rule of the relationship game is, "It's my way or the highway," then I am a bully in that relationship. If the rule is, "It's your way no matter what I want," then I am a wimp. Cooperation requires that I find balance between what I need and what you need. That balance, however, does not have to be exactly equal. If I require absolute fairness, "50% what I need and 50% what you need," then I am a scorekeeper. Being in a relationship is like being on a teeter-totter. A teeter-totter is not much fun if it is stuck in any of three possible positions (up, down, or even) and there is no movement.

The assessment of cooperation is measured by answering three questions. First, does the individual understand the concept of cooperation? Second, how well does the individual balance the skills of speaking and listening? Third, how much does the individual cooperate?

Does the Individual Understand the Concept of Cooperation?

Some individuals do not understand the concept of cooperation. They always get what they want and assume that is how life is and how it is supposed to be. If they do not get what they want from a particular relationship, they leave in search of someone who will meet all of their needs. They have a sense of entitlement. Other people never get what they want and are trapped in unhealthy relationships but do not know that there are alternatives. They believe either that they do not merit obtaining what they desire or that they cannot get what they want, so they settle for less. Still others believe that the only way to be in a relationship is if there is absolute fairness or absolute equality, with each person contributing exactly the same amount. If that equal balance does not occur, such individuals either continuously demand fairness or leave the relationship hoping to find someone who will play by the rules.

These are three examples of people who do not understand what cooperation is. They are bullies, wimps, or scorekeepers. They practice the three foundational skills of speaking, listening, and cooperating in an immature way. These individuals either speak too much, listen too much, or cooperate too much. As a result, if they stay in a relationship, they are destined to develop unhealthy dynamics. If they leave, they will find either ephemeral relationships or unhealthy, codependent dynamics. In the long run, all of these individuals are likely to be unsatisfied and unhappy in their relationships. For many of these people, the problem may lie with a deficit of knowledge. These individuals may not know what cooperation is.

> Jonathan is frustrated. He has been in several short-term relationships, but has never found "the right one." His relationships start out so well, with lots of passion and romance, that he allows himself to believe that "this one" is his soul mate. Sooner or later, however, his dream turns into a nightmare. His partner becomes demanding and controlling. He attempts to give her what she wants, but she only wants more from him. She is never satisfied. Jonathan, in desperation, finally leaves the relationship. He finds another woman. He vows not to allow himself to be "walked all over," so he lays down ultimatums for his new lover. He's "going to be the man of the house." That doesn't seem to work either; the relationship still goes sour. He wonders if he will ever find someone to love.

In the case of a lack of knowledge, clients can benefit from communication skills training, helping them to identify which core skills they already possess and which complementary skills they need to develop. First, they can benefit from training in self-awareness to identify their needs. Second, they can benefit from empathy development, learning how to identify another person's needs. Third, they can be taught the concept of sharing. When people work together to find solutions, each person is enhanced and neither is diminished. Cooperation requires an investment in finding solutions that both people can live with, not just me, and not just you. Cooperation also requires the ability to be flexible and adaptable to the situation, versus rigid and fixed. Many people can benefit from simple explanations of the concept of cooperation. These individuals may have never seen true cooperation in action or may have never understood the concept.

How Well Does the Individual Balance the Skills of Speaking and Listening?

It is relatively easy to discern where an individual is on the cooperation spectrum because an observer can determine the relative balance of speaking and listening behaviors. Cooperation is assessed by ascertaining the relative balance of an individual's ability to speak and listen.

Individuals who know how to cooperate are invested in finding solutions that work. They say what they want, listen to what others want, and keep talking and listening until they find an acceptable result. These individuals and couples will not often come to the therapy room because they are adept at finding solutions. They will be relatively happy because each of their needs is being met through their ability to cooperate.

Individuals and couples who come to our offices will likely either speak up too little or too much, or will listen too little or too much. The assessment process with these individuals will depend largely on whether they come in individually or with their partner. If they come in with their partner, the task will be relatively easy. The therapist can simply ask open-ended questions or assign tasks that will get the couple talking, preferably to one another. For example, "Tell each other what each of you wants from your relationship." Or, "Talk to each other about how you decide how money is spent." The clinician can then simply listen and observe who starts the conversation, the way the speaker talks, how much is said and by whom, how much listening occurs and by whom, and the tone of the conversation between the individuals. The professional versed in the Family Wellness model will easily be able to identify the relative balance of speaking and listening. This is valuable information that will assist the clinician in developing goals and practical interventions to help change the tenor of the communication between couples.

In Chapter 4, I wrote about Jerry, his wife, and their two kids. In the few minutes that he was in my office, I immediately knew that only Jerry's opinion mattered within the family. Although he had acquiesced to their requests that he come to therapy, he only managed to stay for a few minutes. In his family, it was Jerry's way or the highway. Somehow his wife had managed to speak up for herself and get her husband to therapy, but once in the office she reverted to absolute silence. She never said one word during the session. In fact, neither did either of the children. There was no room for cooperation. The family dynamic was so skewed because of Jerry's authoritarianism that the family is at significant risk for domestic violence. That is why I still worry about what became of his wife and the children.

If an individual comes to the office alone, the therapist needs to determine how he or she interacts with significant others. The therapist can ask the client to describe situations in which there is a difference of opinion about important matters (money, sex, the kids, time management, and roles being the top five topics couples argue over) and how those discussions go. The therapist listens to how the individual describes what is said, by whom, and how the statements are expressed. The clinician also listens to how much listening occurs, whether there is evidence of making efforts to understand the words, feelings, and energy of the other, and whether the individual is able to stay focused on the agenda or needs of the other individual.

Also, the therapist can observe the nature of the relationship that the client is able to develop with him or her. Assuming that the therapist establishes a safe environment, develops good rapport, and creates the opportunity for clients to express themselves, it will not take long for clients to recreate, in the therapy office, how they interact with others. Notice if the individual takes a one-down, one-up, or side-by-side position with the therapist. That positioning can be evaluated based on how well the individual is able to balance speaking and listening. Individuals who are healthy are able to speak up adequately without becoming domineering. They are able to listen without becoming overly deferential. The clinician can interrupt the client who is speaking and notice the response. The client may not be able to easily accept interruptions, which can suggest that the client may not be able to cooperate well. On the other hand, the clinician can ask the client who is quiet to speak up. Notice how much the client is able to speak with prompting. An individual who is not able to say much despite being given the opportunity to do so may have difficulty with taking space in a situation in which cooperation is warranted.

Cooperation requires that each person in a dyadic relationship speak up for his needs, listen and care about the needs of the other person, and know how to look for areas of agreement so that a solution can be found that works for both parties. A person who speaks up a lot may need to listen more. A person who listens a great deal may need to speak up more. If both people in a relationship seem to be able to speak up and listen, then the clinician needs to understand how much and how well they cooperate.

How Much Does the Individual Cooperate?

Although it takes two people to make a couple, the couple will only be as healthy as the individual members of that relationship. Each person is responsible to be as emotionally healthy as possible. In the case of cooperating toward solutions that work for both parties, the question of how well an individual cooperates must be answered.

Assuming that both individuals know how to speak up for their needs and how to listen well, if a couple is unable to find mutually satisfactory agreements, the problem may lie in how much the individuals cooperate. Some individuals begin a process of cooperation by stating what they need and want. Then each listens to what the other person needs or wants. After all the cards are on the table, the couple may either prematurely decide to go with one person's goals or the other person's goals. Other couples may continue to discuss and, ultimately, argue about a solution and may never be able to resolve the conflict. A third potential outcome is that the couple requires any solution to be perfectly fair.

In the case of "premature cooperation," one or both individuals choose to not fight. As a result, one person gives in to the needs of the other. That is an acceptable solution on occasion. If, however, that solution is the norm, then the couple has colluded to never fight, or one person in the relationship is not making space for himself, or one person is not allowing space for the other. None of those three possibilities is healthy. The couples I worry about the most in my therapy office are the people who tell me, "We never fight." Those relationships may be quiet for a while and not show outward signs of danger. In fact, others may call them "the ideal couple." Over time, however, the dynamics will intensify until either a major implosion or explosion occurs. These individuals listen too much and need to speak up more. A good, fair fight clears the air and can diffuse difficulties within the relationship. In fact, a healthy fair fight creates intimacy within the relationship by showing each person that despite the occasional conflict, the other person will be there to love them after the dust settles. That security can add to each person's ability to openly discuss his needs without fear of being rejected or abandoned. The net result is more open communication and increased intimacy.

In the case of "delayed cooperation," one or both individuals choose to never give in. They view giving up on their position as capitulation. They believe that if they do not get what they want, then the other person has won. They view cooperation as the art of cutthroat negotiation. They view cooperating as losing and losing as being weak. These individuals are good at speaking up but they are terrible at listening. They may hear the other person's words; they may even understand the emotions behind the words, and also be able to identify the level of energy being expressed. What they are unable to do is to entertain the possibility of actually working together to find a solution that is mutually acceptable. This position reflects the inability to see gray; all situations are either black or white. Such an individual is not able to cooperate because he is afraid that to give any ground will allow the other person to annihilate him. This position may reflect deeply seated issues regarding an inadequate sense of self. Ultimately, failure to cooperate will result in either the end of the relationship or the development of an unhealthy codependency.

In the case of the "perfect consummation," one or both individuals require that any solutions reached be absolutely and perfectly fair. The expectation is that every decision will have an equal outcome for each party. "If you get to go somewhere this week, then I expect to be able to go somewhere next week. If you stayed out 10 minutes later than expected, then I will stay out 10 minutes later the next time I go out." While this approach requires balance and sounds evenhanded, it actually represents an unhealthy level of scorekeeping. Such expectations are immaturely rigid. This is the teeter-totter that must be absolutely balanced. Couples on this teeter-totter are not having much fun. Assessment of this approach to cooperation requires the therapist to listen carefully to the level of flexibility and rigidity demonstrated by one or both individuals when it comes to problem solving. These individuals cannot negotiate a settlement that is more or less acceptable. Instead, they negotiate a settlement that is "not more and not less, or it is not acceptable."

TREATMENT PLANS: FINDING BALANCE BETWEEN SPEAKING AND LISTENING

Assessing how well an individual cooperates allows for the development of a practical treatment plan. There are three types of goals that will likely be established: helping an individual learn how to cooperate, how to cooperate less, or how to cooperate more.

Individuals who already know how to work things out (cooperate) between themselves and the significant others in their lives will likely do so and will not require the services of a mental health professional. They will generally not be referred for counseling because they will use their speaking up skills to make their needs known and their listening skills to connect with others, or they will decide that a particular relationship is untenable and will effect the changes necessary to find peace and tranquility, learning how to live happily ever after with or without that relationship—all without involving a professional third person.

Learning How to Cooperate

As previously noted, people may need to learn to cooperate as the result of a lack of information. Such individuals can get information about what cooperation entails within a therapy setting, within interpersonal support groups, or through psychoeducational classes on communication.

The goals for these individuals are to acquire information about the skills (speaking and listening) and the attitude required to successfully cooperate (negotiating toward a win-win solution), and to get practice in using this new information in their lives.

If an individual learns to cooperate, there is no guarantee that the other person or persons in his life also know how to cooperate or are disposed toward cooperation. Acquiring the tools for cooperation is the goal, even if the tools are used to end a particular relationship. In that situation, the treatment may still be considered successful because it is up to the individual to choose how to use the skill. A decision to end a relationship is just as legitimate as a decision to work toward its improvement. Many individuals find, upon learning how to cooperate, that these new tools enhance their happiness within the relationship, and they find new hope for improving the relationship dynamics.

Learning to Cooperate Less

Some people cooperate so much that they become scorekeepers. They believe that they have a disproportionate amount of responsibility within the relationship. They keep track of everything that they do. They compare the amount that they do to what they consider to be the very little that the other person does. They talk about how tired they are and complain about how relaxed the other person appears. They believe that the other person is relaxed precisely because he does so little. The focus becomes a crusade to right the wrong and balance the score sheet. To find balance, the other person must do much more than his share to make up for the injustices of the past. This immature style of relating stems from a need to have everything in a relationship be exactly equal.

> Julie and Simon had a fun marriage ceremony and an incredible honey-moon in Hawaii. It was a dream event, including island music, hula dancers, a luau, surfing, and everything else that makes that state a paradise for tour-ists. But their relationship became "paradise lost" when they returned home. This was the second marriage for both and each had two children. Although they had thought about bringing the kids to the ceremony, they had de-cided against the plan due to the expense. Over time, the marriage became characterized by frequent arguments about the kids: Both partners felt that their own children were not treated fairly by the other adult. They came for marriage counseling after realizing that they got along extremely well as a couple only as long as they did not talk about the children. Whatever each person did was never "fair enough" when it came to the children.

In stepfamily situations, this perceived imbalance is accentuated when the new couple has children from prior relationships. The complaint is, "You treat your kids better than you treat my kids." This perceived imbal-ance becomes the barrier to forging strong bonds within the new relation-ship.

These individuals have taken a wonderful skill, the ability to cooperate, and have developed an unhealthy and immature focus on making sure ev-erything in the relationship is exactly balanced and fair. The goal for scorekeepers is to focus on what they choose to do and refrain from focus-ing on what the partner does or does not do. Individuals may choose not to do certain things. If so, they can use their speaking up skill to establish boundaries. When people always say yes and never say no to the needs or demands of others, they often become angry, resentful, and bitter. Instead, individuals need to learn when to say yes and when to say no. Establishing these boundaries requires partners to determine what they are willing to do in the relationship. Clients can develop goals for learning how to ef-fectively set limits on what they are willing to do. We cannot change someone else. The other person will decide if he or she wishes to rebal-ance a relationship in a healthy manner. The responsibility for change is with the client, not the other person in the relationship. When an indi-vidual establishes healthy boundaries, it provides the other person with an opportunity to change in order to improve the relationship. Although the ultimate outcome may be uncertain, the goal for recovering scorekeepers is to focus on what they are willing to do and make changes accordingly.

Learning to Cooperate More

Some individuals know how to cooperate but choose not to do so very often. They may be self-focused and may have little interest in understanding the needs of others. The individual may have very little empathy or may understand the needs of the other person but does not care to comply.

Most people in a relationship do not wake up in the morning and make it their life goal to make other people miserable. Most people desire to have a good day and to work together. When cooperation does not occur, assessing what is preventing it may be helpful in establishing a practical treatment plan.

Sometimes, people may not cooperate because they already feel they give in too much. In such cases, they may need to talk with their partner to express their concern. They may also need to listen to their partner in order to learn what the other person believes about their relationship. Others do not cooperate because they do not know how to cooperate. These people need to learn about communication and cooperation. Finally, some individuals do not cooperate much because they are afraid that if they do, they will be taken advantage of and will lose their identity within the relationship. These individuals may need support in understanding that listening to the needs of another does not mean that we must meet their needs or that we must agree with their position. Increased listening and empathy toward the other person may become the goal so that an individual can feel comfortable that in cooperating more he will not lose his individual identity.

Cooperation: Treatment Plans

Helping individuals identify where they are on the cooperation teeter-totter leads to determining appropriate goals for treatment. Remember that it takes two to tango. Actual cooperation requires two healthy individuals. The other person involved in a cooperation dyad may or may not be healthy. We cannot make the other person healthy. Therefore, goals need to focus on what the individual client can do.

The Family Wellness model teaches that cooperation is finding balance between my needs and the needs of others. My needs are legitimate and so are the other person's needs. In the process of cooperation, I speak up for my needs and then listen to your needs. By listening, I do not have to agree with your statements or comply with your demands. Listening is the gift we give to another. We then choose whether to comply with the other's requests. There is no exact balance that needs to be achieved for a relationship to be considered healthy. The exact manner of finding solutions to problems will depend on the people involved in the conversation.

The treatment plan for cooperation needs to include information about how to cooperate and about how much to cooperate. The specific requirements of a particular client will be developed by listening for what happens when the individual is ineffective in cooperating. The more specific the treatment plan is about how and when to cooperate, the better the chance that the individual will accomplish the goals.

The generic treatment plan identifies the presenting or primary issue being addressed. In this chapter, we are concerned about helping people to either learn how to cooperate, to cooperate less, or to cooperate more.

The initial therapeutic task in the development of a treatment plan is to listen to our client's hopes and dreams for the future that are affected by the inability to cooperate well. After the desired outcome has been stated, then all individuals involved in achieving it must be identified. Often the others will include a spouse or significant other, a coworker, a boss, a relative, or a friend. Once they have been identified, a variety of possible solutions can be explored. This process is often referred to as brainstorming. The possible solutions will result in a list of potential interventions, from which one can be chosen by the client. Implementation requires an answer to the question "Who does what by when?" In the case of developing cooperation skills, the answer will almost always be that the client must speak more or less, listen more or less, or make an effort to cooperate more or less. Finally, the question of how progress will be assessed must be answered. Figure 5.1 shows a sample completed treatment plan focused on cooperation.

When people have a forum to speak, when they can trust that the other person will make every effort to hear and understand, then the potential for successful cooperation exists. The skills can be taught. What cannot be taught is whether the other person is trustworthy. The only way to discover the trustworthiness of another is to speak up clearly and then listen carefully. The individual will then be able to ascertain whether it is safe to trust the other person. That decision will, obviously, determine the nature of the relationship into the future.

The ability to cooperate well enhances the intimacy within a relation-

---

FIGURE 5.1
COMPLETED TREATMENT PLAN FOR COOPERATION

- Presenting or primary issue *Spouse and I can never agree on where to go on vacation.*

- Desired outcome *I want to go on a vacation to the Grand Canyon next spring with my spouse for 2 weeks.*

- Who is needed to solve? *Self and spouse only.*
- Brainstorm solutions *Discuss cost for various vacations. List three potential vacation sites. Discuss pros and cons of auto versus air travel.*

- Solution to implement *Tell spouse where I want to go, listen to where spouse wants to go, and keep talking and listening until we come to a solution we both like.*

- Who does what by when? *Saturday, I will tell my spouse where I want to go on vacation. I will ask him to think about it and tell me on Sunday where he wants to go on vacation. We will then begin to discuss our options (taking turns speaking and listening) and we will meet each night after dinner for one-half hour to continue the discussion and negotiation.*

- Date to reevaluate progress *We will meet the following Saturday to finalize our joint decision.*

- Alterations to plan *None at this time. Each weeknight evening, we will each write down anything that seems critical in the decision-making process. I will seek to be very specific about my needs and I will listen more carefully to my spouse's words, feelings, and energy. I will commit to being flexible yet firm.*

---

ship. When individuals know that they can speak up and that they will be
heard and understood, they will trust the relationship and commit more.
Even when a person does not get what he or she wants, the ability to negotiate toward a solution enhances the possibility of risking more because
of the increased trust that occurs through the process of cooperating. It is
especially important to begin practicing cooperation when there have
been difficulties with implementing this skill in the past. Failure to attempt
cooperation means that the individuals involved do not trust the relationship enough to risk and are not using their speaking and listening skills.
When that happens, there is no communication. As a result, there is no
intimacy.

Help clients focus on what they want instead of what they do not want.
Specific goals suggest the practical interventions required to make the
goals reality in the lives of our clients.

PRACTICAL INTERVENTIONS: THE ART OF COOPERATING WITHOUT BECOMING A SCOREKEEPER

People who do not cooperate well need practice. Interventions for enhancing cooperation skills derive from a treatment plan that documents
clear goals. Treatment plans for cooperating better will likely focus on
helping the individual learn how to cooperate, when to cooperate less, or
when to cooperate more.

How to Cooperate

The art of cooperation requires the ability both to speak up and to listen
in a balanced way. After an individual has spoken up for her needs and has
heard the needs of another, a decision must be made. Cooperation is a
choice to continue a dialogue between people who disagree on the desired
outcome but see the conversation through to a successful conclusion. Cooperation requires that an individual be willing to speak up and to listen.
In sum, it is an attitude that seeks the best for all parties involved. The
specific skill required to successfully cooperate is knowing how to negotiate.

People who do not know how to cooperate need an instruction manual.
The Family Wellness model provides that road map. The starting point is
using the word "we"; the path is the ability to alternately speak and listen;

the destination is seeking win-win resolution; and the outcome is increased intimacy.

Helping people learn to cooperate requires that the clinician be actively involved in intervening when an individual demonstrates a lack of capacity. When couples are involved, the therapist must become highly directive. The clinician will ask couples to discuss a difficult topic and will then pay attention to their interaction. When one or the other speaks up too little or too much, or listens too little or too much, or acts as a score-keeper, or demonstrates any other barrier to cooperation, the mental health professional must jump in immediately and begin to coach both individuals in the balanced approach to speaking and listening. While such interruptions are generally unacceptable in polite society, the clinician utilizing Family Wellness training must immediately interrupt and help the person by providing instruction. This process is likened to two people walking on the Grand Canyon Rim Trail. Suddenly, your friend missteps and is about to go down off the edge of the cliff and into the abyss. As the companion, you must immediately respond and get the person back on the safe path. That is partly the task of coaching and that is why we do not believe that clinicians interrupt in that scenario—they intervene.

Helping individuals learn how to cooperate is primarily an instructional task about the two jobs of the individual (to have a good sense of self and to know how to connect with others) and the three skills of the individual (speaking, listening, and cooperating). The Family Wellness model is unique in that it takes extremely complex interactional concepts and translates them into easy-to-understand language. When people are in crisis, those are the words they will remember, understand, and utilize. This educational process can occur in large group settings or within the privacy of the therapist's office. Sometimes an individual will require paper-and-pencil exercises, either through workbooks or other therapeutic aids collected or developed by the clinician. These exercises should focus on the skills of speaking and listening and on the attitude of cooperation.

When to Cooperate Less

Although it seems counterintuitive, some people cooperate too much, which occurs when the desired outcome is absolute fairness. Some people believe that if they get less than their partner in any situation requiring cooperation, they have lost and the other person has taken advantage of them. Such an attitude may be rooted in family of origin issues, difficulty with siblings, past life experiences, and general problems in prior negotiations. Whatever the root, the result is an absolute rejection of gray in the service of black and white. Either I win or I lose. The fear is that I always lose. The only way to avoid losing is by dividing everything absolutely evenly. In the end, such a person becomes a scorekeeper, endlessly worrying about whether someone else is getting a better deal.

A variety of psychotherapeutic interventions can be helpful when focusing on an individual's need for 50-50 resolutions. These interventions generally focus on helping the individual identify the etiology of this need for fairness through discussion of family of origin issues, early childhood experiences especially with siblings and friends, and past unfair experiences. Such interventions can provide insight. Insight alone, however, is insufficient to effect change. Insight alone never cured anyone. What such an individual requires is practice in learning about the gray scale in relationships. Most relationship issues cannot be evenly divided. If we force that concept on our relationships, we will end up dividing the baby in two, as King Solomon suggested. If the other individual in the relationship consistently relinquishes his position and acquiesces to the needs of the partner for the sake of harmony, then that person is cooperating too much as well. Couples in which one or both individuals are scorekeepers will exhibit a codependent relationship that may last a long time but will be very unpleasant for both parties.

One attribute that is often associated with individuals who must always attain 50-50 outcomes is the need to control. Such a need often comes from growing up in familial situations that were chaotic, out of the child's control, or overly perfectionistic. Individuals with such backgrounds do not like surprises. They want to know what is coming next. When they do not know, they get very anxious and controlling. They try to control themselves, their environment, and the people in their environment.

Once the clinician becomes aware that one or both people in a relationship are colluding in a conspiracy of absolute fairness, the clinician must assist the identified patient in becoming more comfortable with approximations of equality. The therapist may help the client think about concepts such as trust and risk. Then the therapist can help the client identify reasons to trust the other person. If such reasons exist, then the therapist guides the individual to take risks by speaking up for what he needs and then listening to the needs of the other. Seeking the best for the other may not mean that the individual gets what he wants every time. Once an individual realizes that the world does not end if a negotiated outcome is not absolutely fair, the person can begin to relax in those situations and can slowly become more comfortable with gray.

When to Cooperate More

Cooperation is absent when one person does not speak up for his needs, when one person does not listen to the other, and when one or both individuals require absolute fairness. What is happening in the dyadic relationship in any of these three situations is an imbalance of the power teeter-totter. Individuals in these situations think of themselves as one-down, one-up, or on an exactly even teeter-totter. One person does not believe himself valuable enough to have an opinion and voice it, or the individual tried to speak up and did not feel heard or understood, or the demand for perfect fairness subverts the need for cooperation.

Individuals who think of themselves in the one-down position will rarely speak up. These individuals need interventions that will help them to know what they want, give them skills for speaking up, and then allow them to practice working together to find solutions. These individuals may require interventions that focus on self-esteem development, speaking up skills utilizing "I" statements, and listening skills using "you" statements.

When an individual notices that decisions are consistently made by one person or the other, it is a signal that more cooperation is needed. If I am the person who always gets my way, I need to listen more. If I am the person who never gets my way, I need to speak up more. If we can never agree or if we always have to perfectly balance decisions, then we need interventions that look for common ground, not necessarily even ground.

SUMMARY

To cooperate well is to connect well. Healthy connection with others requires that individuals have a good sense of self and that they know how to speak up and how to listen, and that they have skills in negotiating for what they want. If I cooperate well, I give myself the best chance of being happy and the other person will also likely be happy. The ability to cooperate is like the ability to dance. Individuals have to know how to lead and how to follow and when to do each. If the music changes, dance partners need to know how to adapt by being flexible and working together to make the dance both fun and beautiful.

Cooperation requires making the covert overt. Cooperation means that each person puts what he or she wants out on the table. After exploring one another's needs, a decision must be reached. The important aspect of cooperation is not necessarily the final decision but the process used to achieve that outcome.

The three skills of speaking, listening, and cooperating are the foundation for a healthy individual and for a healthy relationship. Individuals will likely be good at one skill (speaking or listening) and will need to get better at the other. When both individuals are good at using their skills, they find ways to cooperate and achieve solutions that work. When individuals and couples have a solid foundation of skills, they are ready to build the Family Wellness house. That metaphorical house has three important rooms: equal value for couples and parents in charge of families, room to be close and apart, and expect change (an absolute certainty). That home represents my favorite definition of family: a place to belong and a place to grow.

SECTION III

THREE PATTERNS

6

Equal Value and Parents in Charge

Healthy Couples and Healthy Parents

BEING AN EMOTIONALLY healthy individual provides the best opportunity to be in a healthy relationship. Healthy individuals tend to attract other healthy individuals, and vice versa. The heart of the family is the couple. Many families today are led by single parents or are blended families. The same principles apply to all healthy families: Each person in a relationship is valuable, and families work best when the parents are in charge. In this chapter, we highlight three things that individuals must do to form and maintain a healthy relationship: commit, cooperate, and connect. We then describe the basic principles of healthy parenting.

EQUAL VALUE AND PARENTS IN CHARGE

Equal Value (Healthy Couples)

A basic tenet of the Family Wellness model is the immense importance of each person being an individual with a realistic and positive sense of self, a sense of Me. We know that some people live their lives as singles and do not seek out a romantic, committed relationship. They may instead develop healthy and satisfying friendships throughout life. Most people, however, desire romantic connection with others in general and with one specific other in particular. The second basic tenet of the Family Wellness model is that individuals need to know how to be in relationship with others, to form a We.

COMMIT

First, individuals must commit to themselves. People who like themselves are in a better position to like others for the right reasons. People who have a poor sense of self look for someone to complete them. In those situations, a one-half person often finds another one-half person. Together they form one entity, which seems perfect at first. Unfortunately, that unit easily becomes codependent because one part cannot survive without the other. Romeo and Juliet are often thought of as a model for young love, the epitome of romance. In fact, they represent the tragedy that can happen when individuals are incomplete within themselves and seek to form a more perfect union.

To develop a healthy relationship, each person needs to have both feet firmly planted on the ground. Healthy individuals have a realistic and positive sense of who they are. They make a commitment to being the best they can be by utilizing their speaking, listening, and cooperating skills. Each person expresses his or her needs, hopes, and dreams. Each listens to and cares for the other. Each knows how to play well with others. If an individual has undergone traumas or other experiences that have prevented the development of a realistic and positive sense of self, it is that person's responsibility to seek help in becoming the best he or she can be. Such help may include the services of a mental health professional.

Once individuals are healthy enough, they are prepared to make the commitment to another to form a new relationship. Commitment is the choice to be with someone. A synergy occurs when healthy people unite to live, to love, and to nurture one another. It is a recognition that while "I am good alone, we are better together."

Ted has been married three times in the past. Each relationship started out well, with a honeymoon phase, a discovery phase, a "me" phase, and the ultimate death of the relationship. Ted stated that he came for therapy because while he loved his wife, he was not "in love" with her. He had experienced this situation before. In each relationship, Ted had accommodated himself to the personality of each wife and, in the name of harmony, usually kept quiet about his hopes and dreams. In the end, each relationship ended poorly because each wife did not provide him with the happiness he sought and for which he desperately yearned. Once love died, he returned to the hunt. He sought to find the right one instead of being the right one. Ted was a serial relationship killer not because he was bad or mean but because he was incomplete. He sought to find happiness externally instead of internally. The elusive completion he yearned for was actually within his reach, inside him and not outside. Ted was looking for love in all the wrong places.

Commitment to be with someone, then, begins with a commitment to ourselves to be the best that we can possibly be. We then choose to be with someone else. Notice that while we are looking at romantic love relationships, the same principles apply to friendships. This is why people often say, "I want my spouse to be my best friend." There is not really much of a difference between the two types of connection with others, except that we sleep with our romantic partner and usually do not do so with our friends. Once we choose to be with someone else, we must then negotiate with one another as to how we will be with one another.

COOPERATE

Having committed to ourselves and to another to be as healthy as possible, the next important decision is about how a couple is going to coexist with each other: the nature of the power differential within the couple relationship. The Family Wellness model looks at human relationships in terms of the dynamics between the individuals in the relationship. Family Wellness looks at individuals as being above, below, or beside one another (see Figure 2.3).

An individual who is in the above role is a leader who takes care of others. One in the below role is a follower who is taken care of. Neither role equates to the relative worth of each individual because each person is unique and unquestionably valuable and deserving of respect. In modern Western thought, optimal couple relationships are deemed to be egalitarian in nature. While each person has different strengths and weaknesses, the optimal manner of interaction is generally considered to be beside one another.

Some couples decide that one individual will be above (whether for religious, cultural, or other reasons) and the other person will be in the below role. If the members of a couple agree to that manner of interaction, that is their choice. That dynamic is considered to be a healthy cooperation as long as both individuals discussed it and came to a mutually satisfying agreement. If one person simply takes on the leadership role without the consent of the partner, that person has grabbed power and has become a bully while the other person has either chosen or has been pushed into the wimp role. That style does not demonstrate healthy cooperation. The Family Wellness model accepts that individuals have the right to make their own decisions about their position within the dynamic of a relationship. Individuals are considered to be experts on their lives. Even when the decisions are inconsistent with the norms of a community, the individuals have a right to live their lives as they see fit. The mental health practitioner has to be careful not to impose his or her values on others. The only exception is when individuals, couples, or families make choices that are illegal.

Cooperation requires that each person speak up for what he needs and listen and care about what the other person needs, and that they talk and listen in order to come to decisions that are acceptable to both. An individual will only be capable of cooperation when he understands and appreciates both his own worth and the worth of the other person. The result of such interactions is respect. When people are able to cooperate regarding the relative power differential within a relationship, they will be much better able to cooperate about other issues in their lives. People who cannot cooperate well will likely not be well connected. They will seek only what they want and will not be open to negotiating for the common good. Such relationships yield little intimacy.

CONNECT

The final decision for couples is about how they will stay connected to one another, not only for a little while but for the long haul. Healthy individuals have divergent interest areas, activities, and responsibilities. They know what they want and speak up for it, and they will often get what they want. These individuals work hard, play hard, and live well. Such individuals need to make sure that they stay connected with one another because of the competing demands of time and of other interests.

It is said that love is a decision that we make every day. We demonstrate that love in word and action. Staying connected, likewise, is a choice to spend time and to interact with one another. Healthy connection allows individuals to be close and also to move apart from one another as each engages in separate activities. When couples return from their separate activities, they have more to share with each other due to their unique experiences. The Family Wellness model thinks of connection as the ability to stand together because of each person's ability to stand alone.

Couples need time together to help them sense a continued connection. They need to find common ground and engage in activities that are enjoyable to both. Sometimes, one person in a relationship will love a certain activity that the other person could live without.

> Joe saw Tchaikovsky's *Nutcracker Suite* once with his wife. Joe liked it but he was extremely tired and almost fell asleep about three-quarters through the ballet. His wife loved it so much that she ordered tickets as soon as they were available the following year. Joe went with his wife again. For her, Christmas is not Christmas without seeing this particular ballet. Over the years, Joe has seen the *Nutcracker* in numerous venues, in different cities, and in various versions. He has seen the *Nutcracker* on ice, on skates, by children, by teenagers, by local troupes, by international performers, and in any other way that can be imagined. While he enjoys the music a little and likes the costuming, it seems that he is generally tired about three-quarters of the way through. The last time Joe saw the ballet, he was actually the one who purchased the tickets as a surprise for his wife. Why? Because a couple of years earlier, his wife sat through a major league baseball game with him on her birthday. She likes baseball, but Joe figures that she would have preferred to be somewhere else on her birthday. Joe knows that it works for both of them for him to do something she wants from time to time. It is a way of staying connected. It is a small price to pay for a lifetime of love.

Connection involves doing activities together. It also is about having shared goals and dreams. Connection includes physical, sexual, mental, spiritual, and emotional ways of relating to one another that demonstrate mutual love and respect. Couples who succeed in staying in love and staying together for the long haul do so in large part because they have figured out different ways to stay connected.

Parents in Charge (Healthy Parents)

Once individuals have children, the adults have to decide how they will continue to relate to each other and how they will relate to the children as parents. The Family Wellness model states that parents have to be leaders and models for their children. Families work best when the adults are in charge and when there are clear family roles and appropriate boundaries.

HIERARCHY
Parents have to decide how they will relate to their children. Some parents try to be friends with their children. Others are dictatorial. Still others make the family a democracy, with each person having a vote in the decision-making process. Each of these positions is fraught with peril for

the adults and the children. The Family Wellness model states that parents have two jobs: to be leaders and models.

As leaders, parents make rules, stick together, and stay in charge. As models, parents make time for their children, encourage them, listen to them, and talk together with them. When parents are in their leadership role, they have the authority and responsibility to make rules and enforce consequences, both positive rewards for compliance and negative consequences for noncompliance. Couples need to support each other. Single parents need to have other adults from whom they can draw support and encouragement. It is hard enough to be a parent in a nuclear family. It is even harder to be an effective single parent or a parent in a stepfamily. When parents are modeling for their children, they purposefully lay aside their authority in order to encourage their children to use their speaking, listening, and cooperating skills more effectively. Although individuals tend to be either good leaders or good models, the children need each parent to be good at both jobs.

Healthy families are led by parents who understand that they are in the above position relative to their children and who take their role as leaders seriously. This does not mean that parents are better or more valuable than children, but simply that they have different roles. When parents are not in charge, children will often fill the vacuum and attempt to be in charge, usually with disastrous results. A parent who is good at leading often is not as good at modeling. As a result, the more extreme one parent becomes as a leader or a model, the more extreme the other parent will be in an effort to counterbalance the first parent's position.

Healthy families understand the importance of hierarchy. Hierarchy asserts that parents are in charge of a family. It reflects the differing levels of authority within a family. The parents set and enforce the standards of behavior for the children. The standards are based on the values and beliefs of the parents. For a hierarchical family structure to be successful, two elements are required: complementarity and flexibility/adaptability.

Complementarity means that the adults accept their interdependence. They agree to work together as a team, to give and get cooperation, and to blend their perspectives, their skills, and their styles for the benefit of the couple relationship as well as for the family. They model the three skills of speaking, listening, and cooperating. As a result, the children benefit from the safety that is inherent in healthy families where the parents work together for the common good.

Flexibility/adaptability refers to the importance of a family's organization and structure gradually changing in response to the changing needs of the members of the family. The family must be ready to change while remaining stable. The bonds of the family must be elastic like a rubber band and cannot be unyielding like manacles. Families that are overly fluid become chaotic and symptomatic. Families that are overly rigid become symptomatic as well.

The job of parents as leaders and models is to accept the above role in terms of taking care of their children. They do so by making appropriate rules that support their values, staying connected to support their common goals, and enforcing consequences by rewarding compliance and allowing natural and logical consequences as well as supplying additional consequences for noncompliance. The adults embrace their role as co-leaders and take a beside position with one another. The children acknowledge and accept their below role and follow rules. Everyone realizes that families work best when everyone does their job.

FAMILY ROLES

The ties that bind families are based on mutual need. Children need to be taken care of. Parents need to take care of children. Partners need to care for one another. Family members are constantly striving to meet the needs for security, safety, expression, and belonging. Each person is expected to use speaking, listening, and negotiating skills in efforts to meet needs and to secure a portion of the available familial resources. As such, families are not stagnant. They are living entities that are constantly adapting to the needs of the individuals within the family as well as to the needs of the family as a whole. The interdependence that occurs in harmonious families develops as a result of people understanding, accepting, and fulfilling their individual family roles in a balanced manner.

The roles of each person can be thought of as organizationally stemming from an above, below, or beside position. Each person within a family may, at different times, be in each position. For example, parents are being parents when they are in the above (taking care of) role. On the other hand, a parent may choose to be in a beside role (as when being a model with a child and listening to the child). A parent may also choose to be in the below role (as when learning from children). Individuals who only know how to be in one of the three roles limit the possibility for personal growth and development. It is important, for example, for parents to learn from their children how to have fun. It is also important for children to learn from their parents how to be responsible. It is through appreciating the differing roles of children and adults in a family that each person's life is enhanced and developing a stronger, healthier family is made possible.

BOUNDARIES

Boundaries are the underlying rules that govern how each member of a family acts: who is allowed to be close to whom, what they can do together, when, and under what conditions. The establishment of boundaries occurs through the interactions between members within the family. Individuals determine what they can and must do in order to get their needs met in relationship to other individuals within the family. Healthy families have rules that allow each member of the family to be close and to be separate from one another. These rules allow for safety, physical comfort, emotional support, time alone, and participation in family life.

These boundaries are developed in dyadic relationships. Typical boundary rules exist around a husband and wife or similar romantic relationship, the adults as parents, parent and child, and sibling relationships. These rules are often unexpressed but, nonetheless, are very clear about what is acceptable and what is not acceptable between interacting people within the family.

Healthy boundaries exist when individuals are able to get their needs met, are able to be close or apart, and are flexible, and when relationships are mutually satisfying. In healthy families, individuals are able to express themselves to get their needs met, listen to others to hear what they need, and are able to find solutions that work for the parties involved. Healthy dyads within the family are able to solve problems by themselves, or they are able to ask for outside help.

Some families do not have skills that allow for healthy dyadic interactions. These disorganized families may be led by adults who grew up in families which lacked healthy interactions. As a result, they did not learn what healthy interactions look like and were not able to organize their family well. When families get stuck in unhealthy interactions, symptoms develop. The good news is that healthy patterns can be learned, disorganized ways of being can be organized, and families can achieve higher levels of cooperation. Families that are organized well understand and exhibit healthy boundaries between the two-person dyads within the family.

ASSESSMENT: ABOVE, BELOW, OR BESIDE?

Couples and families organize themselves in many ways. How they organize themselves is the idiosyncratic product of individual history, personality, and life circumstances. A quick assessment of that organization will assist the therapist in helping clients develop goals and intervention strategies that promise to improve their lives.

Equal Value (Healthy Couples)

Couples in many Western cultures strive to achieve egalitarian relationships. While not everyone agrees that couples ought to be equal, the Family Wellness model has a core belief that each person within a couple relationship is of equal value. How they choose to express that equality is up to the members of that relationship. A quick assessment of a couple is possible by looking at how committed they are to the relationship, how well they are cooperating, and how well they are connected.

COMMIT

The commitment in a relationship starts with a commitment to self. Individuals will not likely engage in a healthy relationship if they are not taking good care of themselves. A couple is only as healthy as the weakest link. The clinician, therefore, can evaluate how well clients take care of themselves to develop clues about the relative health of relationships. Ask questions such as, "What do you do for fun? What are your hobbies or interest areas? How do you spend your time? What is one thing you recently did that was just for you?" Individuals who are not able to quickly state what they do for self may have difficulty connecting with others in a healthy manner.

Look for how well individuals are able to speak up for their interests, whether they are able to listen and care for others, and how decisions are made by a couple.

Commitment also involves the ability to choose, on a daily basis, to be with someone. Some people have made a choice to be with someone at some point in the past. In the present, they are not sure about that commitment. These people often say, "I love my spouse, but I'm not in love with my spouse." These individuals have one foot in the relationship and one foot out. They may have a room at Mom's house where they can go whenever they want; they may have an insurance policy that lists a daughter from a prior relationship as the beneficiary; they may have money stashed away without their partner's knowledge; or they may engage in behaviors that undermine the marital relationship (such as dating others). Exploring individuals' level of commitment is about how firm they are about being with their partner, in the present and for the future. Do they indicate, "I choose" or do they intimate, "I chose"? Any evidence of current reservations about the relationship or about their partner must be taken into consideration in determining how committed an individual is to the couple relationship.

Choosing to be with another person in a romantic relationship is an individual decision, not one made by committee. Listen to whether a client speaks about his own commitment to the marriage or relationship or about what the partner expects from him. The assessment of commitment is basically a determination about whether the individual is currently choosing to be with the partner, be with someone else, or be with no one.

COOPERATE

Once people have chosen to be together, they must work out many issues cooperatively. They have to decide big things, such as where to live, and little things, such as what to have for dinner. How they decide is of major importance in assessing how well a couple cooperates.

The Family Wellness model proposes that all people in relationships can be thought of as being above, below, or beside in terms of authority and responsibility. People who are above or below are either taking care of or being taken care of. Above or below role relationships may also represent superior or subordinate roles. In the extreme, relationships may represent bully and wimp dyads. They never represent a dynamic of more value or less value because each person is thought of as being equally valuable.

Exploring with an individual or a couple how decisions are reached will yield valuable insight into the nature of the couple's relationship. If both people are available for interview, ask each individual the same question about how specific decisions are made. Evaluate the similarity or disparity of their responses. If only one person is available for interview, ask the same question but keep in mind that the answer will reflect how that person believes the dynamic works. Nevertheless, important information can be gained by listening to how the person describes the other individual and the decision-making process. Listen for subtle cues that reveal whether the individual feels inferior or superior in relation to the other person.

Listen for whether the person appears helpless in making any decisions or feels entitled to make all or most decisions.

Think of a teeter-totter and listen for where individuals place themselves. They often will say that they feel one-down, that they never make decisions. Interestingly, if both people are available for interview, both may tell you that they feel one-down. In such a case, both cannot be one-down on a teeter-totter at the same time. This may mean that they take the lead in different areas and the one who is not making a particular decision feels one-down in that instance. It may mean that they are not communicating well regarding how decisions are made and each one feels left out of the decision-making process. Often, both individuals feel overwhelmed by having to be "the responsible one."

Ultimately, how a couple solves problems reveals the power differential within the couple relationship. Assess the relative amount of speaking versus listening that each person in a relationship exhibits. People who speak up a lot are generally leaders. People who listen a lot are generally followers. Individuals tend to be one or the other. In evaluating a couple relationship, look for whether questioning reveals an individual who appears to be consistently either up or down in the relationship. Explore that issue openly with your client to help determine the appropriate goals. Normally, individuals who are actually in a one-down position need to practice their speaking up skills. People in a one-up position need to practice their listening skills. Sometimes, people speak up well and listen well but are nevertheless dissatisfied with how decisions are made. In these situations, additional training and practice may be required for taking turns in speaking and listening (traffic control) and in developing problem-solving strategies.

Couples who cooperate well generally have mutually satisfying relationships because each person's needs are being met, although not necessarily at the same time. They have learned how to reach solutions that work for both of them. They generally express happiness with the intimate connection between the two of them. Explore with couples how well they know each other and how well they meet each other's needs. Some couples may have gone through very difficult times in their relationship and have, through cooperation, found solutions. Intimacy is often a positive outcome of intense conflict. Conflict in and of itself does not mean that a couple does not cooperate well. The pivotal question is, "How does this couple resolve conflict?" Intimacy is the reward for finding solutions and is the end result of cooperation.

CONNECT

The ultimate goal of a committed relationship is not necessarily just staying together. The desire of most people's hearts is not simply longevity in
a relationship; it is to have fun together, to enjoy one another, and to
grow as individuals while sharing life together. If a couple is going to stay
connected, they have to find a variety of ways to engage with one another
in life.

The assessment of a couple's connection involves asking about activities that they share, interest areas that they have in common, how much
time they spend with each other, what they do together, and so on. Erst-
while philosopher and major league baseball player Yogi Berra once said,
"You can observe a lot by watching." This observation was never truer
than when assessing couples. Couples will physically show you how close
or distant they are by where they sit in your office. Physical distance reveals emotional distance. Proximity reveals intimate connection. Observe
by watching.

Couples who are unable to identify things that they do together for fun
are not likely to be strongly connected. Some couples do things that are
enjoyable to only one party. When that happens consistently, the couple
has likely developed a bully-wimp relationship. The goal for these couples
is to encourage more movement on the teeter-totter. Exact interventions
will depend on where the clients are seated on the teeter-totter. The assessment process seeks to identify the relative position of each person in
the relationship in terms of authority and responsibility as well as in what
the couple does to stay connected.

Couples wherein the individuals have committed to a relationship, who
have learned to cooperate, and who have stayed connected to one another
have found a secret garden: a place to belong and a place to grow.

Parents in Charge (Healthy Parents)

Choosing to be in a relationship is the end of the single life. It is also the
beginning of a new adventure that the couple will experience and cocreate
in their next chapter of life. Becoming a parent is not only another chapter, it is another volume. Being a parent is not for wimps. The pay is terrible, the job is horrendous, the preparation is minimal, and the resources
are almost nonexistent—yet the rewards are amazing.

From a Family Wellness perspective, assessing an individual's capacity
as a parent involves determining how well he or she functions in the dual
roles of leader and model.

PARENTS ARE LEADERS

Parents are leaders when they make rules, stick together, and stay in charge. This role can be very rewarding and equally frustrating. The rewards come from successfully establishing rules that stem from parental values, mutually supporting one another—or learning to obtain support in the case of single parents—and seeing the establishment of a safe and sane family environment where children understand what is expected and cooperate with the program. The frustrations come from feeling inadequately prepared for the job, having divergent perspectives between the parents or with other adults about how to parent, and attempting to guide the family while experiencing a "mutiny on the *Bounty*" on a regular basis. The parent leader can feel like he or she is trying to herd kittens. Assessing an individual's ability to be a leader within the family begins with determining if that person knows how to make rules, followed by being able to cooperate with any other invested adults, and staying in charge. In order to assess these arenas, the therapist needs to look at how well the individual understands and practices the dynamics involved in hierarchy, family roles, and boundaries.

A parent who is a leader has accepted the absolute fact that families work better when parents are in charge. The leader realizes that adults have to make rules and that it is up to children to follow those rules. The parents stay in charge by developing a combination of negotiable and nonnegotiable rules. It is up to the parent to decide which rules are negotiable and which are not. When the rules are not negotiable, the adult stays in charge by making very specific rules, chooses and consistently enforces rewards and consequences, includes children in the process when appropriate, tells children what the rules are, and checks for understanding. Once a rule is concisely developed, clearly communicated, and consistently enforced, the parent has the best chance of having the child do what is expected.

Through the process of establishing and enforcing rules, the parent maintains leadership by recognizing and accepting the responsibility of being a leader for the family. When there are two parents, even when they are not together, it is important for the adults to use their speaking, listening, and cooperating skills to work together on behalf of the children by supporting each other even when they disagree. In severely caustic divorced coparent situations, the adults have to love their children more than they hate their ex-spouse.

Evaluate parents' capacity for being leaders by asking questions about the role of parents, the function of rules within the family, how rules are developed within the home, and what kinds of rewards and consequences are appropriate for parents to utilize within the family. Ask about when and how children should speak up about changing familial rules, how the couple works together when they disagree about a rule or about rewards for compliance and consequences for noncompliance, and what they believe to be the most important factors in a family working together. Finally, ask about the ground rules for dyadic relationships involving closeness and distance. Answers to these probing questions will illuminate for the clinician how the individual thinks about the hierarchical relationship between parents and children, the role relationships, and the boundaries within families.

PARENTS ARE MODELS

Parents are models when they plan time with their children, encourage them, listen to them, and talk together with them. This role can be a great deal of fun as adults and children learn to play together, develop traditions, show love in action, and spend time with one another. This role is exhibited when adults encourage children by identifying their successes and praising their accomplishments and strengths. This is a time to listen to children even when you disagree with them. Parents as models show children that they are valuable, as kids see themselves in the reflection of the parent's eyes. Being a model is also a time to encourage children to grow in relationship with adults, as children learn more about the adults and as adults learn more about the children.

Parents who are models deliberately lay down their role as leaders temporarily in order to have a side-by-side relationship with their children. Because children learn from their parents by watching and imitating, it is important that parents balance being leaders with being models. While parents will always be in an above role because under all circumstances parents need to take care of the children, adults choose to play together with children so that children appreciate their worth and value. It is often the case that children teach adults how to play. When kids teach parents, the children realize that they have something of value to offer their parents. The adult establishes routines and rituals and plans time to be with each child.

When parents encourage their children, they praise efforts and identify any successes or partial successes. They identify specific things that please them about their children and communicate that clearly to them. Children are encouraged to speak up about their goals, hopes, and dreams about the future. Children are encouraged to talk about what matters to them. Parents listen, even when it hurts—and it will. When parents take the risk to encourage children to talk, children will say things that run counter to the parents' values and goals. When we listen, we need to keep our thoughts to ourselves. Remember, listening does not equal agreement. Finally, parents as models have open discussions wherein they talk about their lives and listen to their children. Children are encouraged to become involved in decision making as they develop increasing capacity to make informed decisions about their lives. This is another time when parents tend to revert to being leaders, to telling kids what to do and what not to do. Parents must resist this temptation to assist children in developing their capacity for reason, judgment, and decision making.

Evaluate parents' capacity for being models by asking questions about whether and when it is appropriate for parents to play with their children. Probe about the routines and rituals that parents have with their children, how they ensure that each child feels loved and valuable within the family, and about how children learn values from parents. Ask parents about what they do to ensure that children have a voice within the family and what happens when children say outrageous things that run counter to the parental values on topics such as sex, drugs, alcohol, gangs, bullying, same-sex relationships, domestic violence, and so on. Finally, ask parents to tell you under what circumstances they should be open about their past or their values. Responses to these answers will yield valuable information about how individuals view the role of parents as models.

TREATMENT PLANNING: COUPLES AS PARTNERS
AND PARENTS AS LEADERS

Assessment naturally leads to treatment planning. Individuals stuck in a below or above position with their romantic partner, or in a friendship, need skills to develop flexibility while generally being in the optimal beside position.

Individuals who do not demonstrate healthy leadership to their children need to develop leadership skills, which include being a leader and being a model.

The mental health professional's job in treatment planning is to, in concert with the client, develop a substantive treatment plan to improve the individual's ability to engage in mutually satisfying partner relationships and to help parents to guide their children through clear and flexible leadership.

Equal Value and Equal Power

A basic tenet of the Family Wellness model is that all individuals have worth and value. People are not better or worse than others because of their socioeconomic status, their educational level, their looks, or any other measures of success. People are valuable for being who and what they are: human beings. When people engage in couple relationships, they first choose to be with someone; then they determine the nature of the power differential between them (consciously or subconsciously). The decision about how a Me will be as a We usually depends on how each individual in the dyad thinks and feels about himself or herself.

LEARNING TO BE ME AND WE

Individuals ideally have a realistic and positive sense of self. Often, the people that the therapist sees are individuals who have inadequate or inflated beliefs about themselves. People with an inflated sense of self are not likely to come to the therapist's office unless they have been mandated to do so by law enforcement or by a spouse. Most of the time, a therapist is dealing with individuals who devalue themselves, who have an inadequate sense of self.

One of the most important things that a mental health professional does for clients is to give them the opportunity to see themselves for whom and what they are: valuable. We were reminded in Chapter 1 that the sense of self usually develops as an individual sees himself or herself reflected in the parent's eyes. Often that image is distorted because of the parent's issues related to stress, mental illness, emotional instability, substance abuse, depression, or some similar condition that prevents a true reflection of who the child is. The therapist may be one of the few individuals in a client's life who has ever made a concerted effort to accurately reflect the client's worth and value back to the client. Naturally, the clinician must share the Family Wellness vision of the basic worth of all individuals, what Carl Rogers described as unconditional positive regard.

When an individual feels inadequate, the goal is to develop a realistic and positive sense of self. This generic goal needs to be specified based on the needs of the individual. Sometimes the issue is body image; sometimes it is intellectual deficits (actual or perceived); sometimes the person has experienced serial disappointments in relationships; or a myriad of other reasons that have led the client to feel inadequate.

When individuals are not well grounded in who they are, they often develop unhealthy relationships. It is similar to standing on one foot and feeling unsteady. We often grab onto something for support. That person or thing may assist us temporarily but will cause us to be unbalanced over time. We become dependent or codependent when we require another to lend us stability. The goal for healthy couples is to become interdependent.

A sample treatment plan for an inadequate sense of self was developed in Chapter 1. In this section, we complete a treatment plan for an inflated sense of self (Figure 6.1). The skills required are increased listening and learning to cooperate. When a person learns to be Me, the individual is in a better position to develop a healthy We.

Once I have a realistic and positive sense of who I am, I am in a better position to develop healthy relationships. Treatment plans sometimes deal with issues of couple enmeshment. This occurs with individuals who have an inadequate sense of self and require the other individual to be with them at all times. Neither individual does anything without the other. Their world becomes increasingly small. Such individuals need to reclaim their individual identity.

Some individuals are codependent. Neither can make a decision without the other. If one of them falls, both of them fall. They are like half an individual connected to another half, which equals one. The problem is that we are talking about two individuals, not one. These individuals need to reclaim their identity and need to learn how to make decisions on their own and in their own best interests, not just the needs of the other. Treatment goals may include learning that taking care of self is not selfish, establishing boundaries, and learning to make independent choices.

Parents in Charge

In modern society, the autocratic parenting style of demanding absolute obedience to parents does not work very well. On the other hand, the democratic style of "one person, one vote" does not work either. Since 1980, the Family Wellness model has proposed that families work best when parents are both leaders and models.

LEARNING TO BE LEADERS AND MODELS

Parents who are leaders demonstrate leadership by making clear and specific rules for what they want. These parents stick together with their spouse or other important adults and work together. They stay in charge

FIGURE 6.1
COMPLETED FAMILY WELLNESS TREATMENT PLAN
FOR INFLATED SENSE OF SELF

- Presenting or primary issue   *Spouse thinks I'm a know-it-all.*
- Desired outcome   *I want myself and my spouse to have dynamic conversations wherein we both express our views.*
- Who is needed to solve?   *Self and spouse only.*
- Brainstorm solutions   *Discuss only "safe" topics.*
  Take turns listening and talking.
  Discuss things at a low to medium volume.
- Solution to implement   *Do more listening. Make a date with spouse for this Thursday night. Ask spouse to pick a topic she would like to discuss. Listen to spouse fully, to the words, feelings, and energy. Ask spouse if I clearly understand. Express my view. Listen to spouse's response. Listen more. Listening does not equal agreement.*
- Who does what by when?   *Tonight, I will ask my spouse for a date for Thursday night to have a conversation. I will take care of any chores, turn off the television, telephone, radio, and Internet, and complete any other errands early in order to ensure a distraction-free environment. We will then begin to discuss the topic spouse chose. If spouse is reticent to start, I will ask spouse to begin the conversation as I am practicing my listening skill. We will take turns speaking and listening, with me focusing more on listening. At the end of the conversation, I will thank my spouse for taking the time to have the conversation with me.*
- Date to reevaluate progress   *We will meet the following Saturday morning, after breakfast, to discuss our last date. I will ask spouse to pick a movie and we will set a time for our next date.*

FIGURE 6.1
COMPLETED FAMILY WELLNESS TREATMENT PLAN
FOR INFLATED SENSE OF SELF (*CONTINUED*)

- Alterations to plan

None at this time. I will work hard on listening to my spouse's opinions, including the words, feelings, and energy she expresses, in order to demonstrate that I value her insights. I will recognize that even though we may disagree, I am not necessarily right all the time. I will frequently express my appreciation of my connection to my spouse, through words such as, "Thank you for choosing to spend time with me."

---

by making sure that rules are obeyed and people are held accountable for their jobs within the family. The skill required to be a leader is primarily the speaking up skill. Consistent leadership will often result in sufficient structure that promotes harmonious functioning within the family.

Treatment planning for improved leadership is usually focused on the parents being more specific and clear about the expectations for children (Figure 6.2). Another area that often requires reinforcement is for the adults to work together as a team on behalf of the children. A third area that causes difficulties for parents is the consistent application of rewards and consequences for compliance and noncompliance.

Parents who are models show leadership through the way they treat others within the family. They establish routines and rituals and make time to play with their children. These parents encourage their children, listen, and talk together with their children. They make family an enjoyable place to be.

Treatment planning for improved modeling is usually focused on the parents being more actively involved with their children in situations when the parents do not have to stay in charge (Figure 6.3). These parents often have to learn how to lay down their leadership mantle and allow themselves to be playful and temporarily not in charge. Some parents are so good at being models that they need to be encouraged to assume leadership. When parents are models, listening is the skill they are using more. The older children get, the more that parents need to listen.

FIGURE 6.2
COMPLETED FAMILY WELLNESS TREATMENT PLAN
FOR PARENTAL LEADERSHIP

- Presenting or primary issue   *Children rarely obey parental rules.*
- Desired outcome   *I want children to go to bed at their bedtime.*

- Who is needed to solve?   *Self, spouse, and children.*
- Brainstorm solutions   *Be specific about bedtime. Identify clear rewards and consequences. Spouses will support each other with rewards and consequences.*

- Solution to implement   *Couple agrees to a 9:30 p.m. bedtime during the week and 11:00 p.m. on weekends. Tell child what the rule is. Tell child that after one week of going to bed on time the child will earn an extra 30 minutes to be used on an agreed-upon night the following week. If the child does not comply, the child will have to go to bed immediately, will have to get up 10 minutes earlier the next morning, and will have to go to bed 10 minutes earlier the following night. Future noncompliance will increase the number of days the punishment is meted out and will result in other privileges being lost.*

- Who does what by when?   *Parents will discuss exact time for bedtime and will find agreement. A family meeting will be called to implement the new bedtime. As this rule is nonnegotiable, parents will not listen to their children about this topic and will proceed with rewards and consequences. Either parent can enforce.*

people in her life had told her: that she was not worth much. Ultimately, Veronica's self-hatred came to a violent end within the context of an unhealthy domestically violent relationship.

The tale of the two Veronicas demonstrates that making an adequate assessment of an individual requires careful questioning that looks underneath the obvious. Things are not always as they seem—in fact, they seldom are. This is especially true when the topic is low self-esteem.

GOOD SENSE OF SELF

Many people understand their self-worth as emanating from a combination of who they are, what they do, and what they seek (their transcendent values). Healthy people align how they think, how they feel, and what they do in a way that is harmonious and results in what they consider to be their character. These people appreciate that, whether they had a wonderful upbringing or had hard times earlier in life, they are responsible for who they are in the present. They neither aggrandize themselves for their strengths nor deprecate themselves for their weaknesses. They have a quiet, serene sense of self. They appreciate their strengths and acknowledge their deficits. They choose to focus on what is working without losing sight of what needs to be improved.

People with a good sense of self are less likely to seek treatment. Therapists, however, sometimes assess individuals with good self-esteem because they come to the therapist's office due to circumstances beyond their control or because of life choices they are thinking about pursuing. Clinically, therapists are usually dealing with issues such as the death of a loved one, career choices, academic goals, romantic relationship choices, and other life-affirming pursuits. For example, a client may be applying for a certain position that requires psychological evaluation, such as police officer or ordained clergy. Although formal assessment instruments are usually required in such evaluations, a clinical decision also needs to be made based on direct interview. Formal psychological testing instruments should never stand alone.

The Family Wellness definition of healthy self-esteem can assist in this assessment process by clarifying what questions to ask. It is important to correctly assess a client's sense of self, because you may rule out any treatment recommendations about building a realistic and positive sense of self—which is what healthy individuals generally already have. Some practical questions and areas to explore include the following:

1. *Tell me about your strengths.*

   Provide individuals with the opportunity to describe what they do well. Look for the ability to discuss their strengths in terms of intelligence, willingness to work, self-starter qualities, ability to problem solve, and interpersonal skills. Healthy individuals know that it is important to talk about their abilities without exaggerating them. Check to see that an individual is able to state his strengths yet shows some moderation in his description. Check for false modesty. The ability to differentiate speaks volumes about the clinician's capacity to listen carefully to words and also to nonverbal communication.

2. *Tell me about your weaknesses.*

   Provide individuals time to discuss what they see as areas that need improvement. People who are unable to describe any areas of weakness may lack introspection or may be overly enamored with themselves. People who talk about their numerous problems may be honest yet may also lack appropriate boundaries related to social propriety. Such clients may have extremely low self-esteem and may focus excessively on their negative traits. Look for a balance between the ability to speak about strengths and to speak concisely about weaknesses.

3. *Tell me about your goals.*

   Individuals with a healthy sense of self are generally forward looking. They have often achieved prior goals and are constantly constructing new ones. They have dreams, some of which they turn into goals. People with a good sense of self stay busy building the staircase that will allow them to reach their goals. They turn goals into reality.

   Individuals who have difficulty in formulating goals or speaking about goals may have lowered self-esteem due to problems with self-efficacy. They have not achieved and are, therefore, doubtful about future achievement. Or they have achieved and are worried about being able to replicate their successes. In either event, these individuals are tentative when discussing future goals. Carefully listening to individuals discussing their goals can provide valuable assessment information. Listen for the ability to state goals, the specificity of the goals, and the motivation to succeed by pursuing the identified goals.

Individuals with healthy self-esteem are often very responsive to assessment questions without becoming defensive. They will also know when to erect appropriate boundaries. As in most things, look for balance.

INFLATED SENSE OF SELF

A person with an inflated sense of self does not often seek outside help. After all, he already knows the answers to life's issues. No outside professional will have anything of value to offer. Nevertheless, practitioners sometimes meet people with an inflated sense of self because they are the spouse, parent, or child of those already in treatment. The overconfident may be referred for treatment by those clients. Such individuals may also seek help because they want confirmation from the therapist that they are correct and that others are misguided. Individuals with an inflated sense of self may complain that other people in their lives do not appreciate, or even recognize, their strengths and virtues. Therapists may also see such a person because he or she is seeking an occupational position that requires formal evaluation of their ability to function in that position.

> Ramon knew that he was good looking. He also knew that he was smart and funny. He had plenty of friends and enjoyed his work. At home, he was frustrated because his wife did not seem to enjoy having intimate sexual contact with him. He came to therapy because his wife was in therapy. He was confused about her difficulties with sexuality. He assumed that she had a problem and was likely "frigid." His wife revealed that although Ramon was very good in bed, from a mechanical perspective, he seemed to be in another world when he was having intercourse with her. He seemed to be more focused on what he was doing and on himself than on her. As a result, she found their lovemaking to be a chore. It was all about him, despite his efforts at pleasuring her.
>
> Ramon revealed that he always did everything extremely well and so he also wanted to be excellent in bed. As a result, he approached the task of making love as he approached other endeavors in his life. He learned that he needed to focus and attend to the task to be successful. He did focus and attend to the task at hand, and he did it well. However, Ramon was unable to move from his extremely strong sense of self and focus on his wife's needs. Although he made every effort to meet her needs, he was really focused on being superior at his task. As a result, there was no emotional connection during this most intimate of endeavors.

Occasionally, therapists see children with an inflated sense of self who come to treatment because they have not achieved their own expectations of themselves. As a result, they have a "meltdown" and implode, that is, they may develop severe affective symptoms, exhibit dramatic somatic complaints, or become incapable of initiating problem-solving behaviors.

> Jason had been told by his parents, relatives, teachers, and coaches that he was awesome. He was good at sports and he was bright. He usually achieved to a superior degree in whatever sport he engaged. When he occasionally came across an activity that was difficult, he chose to stop playing that sport because he "did not have time" or because he "wanted to do something else." Jason never thought that he quit because he could not do it or could not do it well. Rather, he moved on, in his mind, because he did not "want" to do it.
>
> Jason came to therapy because he experienced what his parents called an "emotional breakdown." In talking with this high school sophomore, it came out that he had received a bad grade for the first time in his academic career. It was an A– in science. He was distraught and blamed the teacher. Obviously, she had done a poor job of telling the class what was expected. He attempted to do extra credit work but was refused the opportunity. In the end, he imploded and had an emotional meltdown.

At first glance, I thought that Jason's parents were likely guilty of projecting unrealistically high expectations onto their child. I was in a difficult spot as Jason's therapist. Should I tell this youngster that he should lower his expectations? What if he did and felt better but failed to achieve his potential? After further discussions with him and with his parents, I was surprised to learn that it was not parental expectations that were at fault for Jason's frazzled emotional state. It became apparent that Jason had developed an inflated sense of self because he had always been told he was great, wonderful, and perfect. Even when he struck out in a baseball game, his parents and others in the stands screamed, "Good job!" He had introjected a concept of self that did not allow for imperfection. When confronted with a less than perfect grade that was, from his perspective, totally unwarranted, he could not deal with it.

Whether people have low self-esteem or an inappropriately inflated sense of self, we assess them by comparing their self-assessment with others' perspectives and with objective reality. Some questions and areas to explore with individuals for the purpose of assessment include the following:

1. Tell me about your weaknesses.

   Listen for any minimization, rationalization, and externalization. To minimize is to diminish the seriousness of any weaknesses or to speak only about a few areas of weakness and to desire to speak only about strengths. Rationalization relates to reluctantly speaking about weakness and then making it clear that any weaknesses have understandable reasons for existing. For example, "I did poorly on a test because I was distracted because I didn't have enough sleep . . . ," or "because I was doing something else that matters more . . . ," or "because I did not care about the project." Take your choice of rationalizations. Externalization occurs when, after reluctantly admitting that a task may have been done poorly, there are many people other than the self to blame for the negative outcome. For example, "The teacher was not clear about what was going to be on the test . . . ," "There was too much noise in the room because the teacher is unable to control the classroom . . . ," or "My friends kept me up all night." Again, take your pick of who is to blame (not including self).

2. Who has helped to make you successful?
   Listen for egocentrism and narcissism. People with an overly inflated sense of self often fail to recognize how others have helped them to achieve what they have accomplished. They believe that who they have become is entirely of their own doing. They tend to take full credit for hard work, intelligence, and other skills and abilities that are self-aggrandizing and tend to diminish the role others have played in their success.

3. Who can help you become a better individual? How can they help?
   People with an inflated sense of self sometimes pay lip service to the hypothetical concept of "always seeking to improve." However, when pressed for specifics, they are not really sure that improvement is necessary. Even if improvement is possible, they do not believe that anyone can actually help them to improve. Such a perspective is well beyond positive self-esteem—it reveals a sense of having achieved the pinnacle and being unable to see how improvement is necessary or possible. This sense of self is destined to create personal and interpersonal problems when reality clashes with the surreal, leaving frustration and devastation in its wake.

Summary

The assessment of the sense of self is extremely complex because the therapist must take into consideration what people reveal about themselves as well as things that they would like to hide from others. The therapist must listen carefully to the words being said, the body language being demonstrated, and the aspects of personal history that impact an individual's personality and manner of being in the present. The therapist must remember that an individual's manner in the present is the result of past experiences. How the person will be in the future is, in part, the product of who the individual is in the present. While each of us is a product of the past, the good news is that we do not have to be prisoners of the past.

The Family Wellness model provides a clear set of concepts about understanding self. The proposition is that an individual needs to have a realistic and positive sense of self. If the concept of self is unrealistically low or high, no matter how it got to be that way, the individual will likely have impediments in the capacity to function effectively in life. It is the therapist's task to help individuals think about themselves in a realistic manner, based on obtaining all of the available information. Once people are thinking realistically, it is important for them to think positively about themselves. Whether to think positively or negatively is a choice. The Family Wellness model posits that people tend to achieve more when they think well of themselves. Realistic and positive thinking becomes a self-fulfilling prophecy.

TREATMENT PLANNING

Treatment planning is the piece of people helping that occurs between assessment and intervention. Treatment planning is the natural outcome of a relatively complete assessment of the person or situation. Once the critical factors that require intervention are known, the clinician in concert with the client formulates a specific set of goals or outcomes that is known as the treatment plan. These goals or desired outcomes may be short, medium, or long term in nature and focus.

Treatment planning regarding an individual's sense of self requires that the practitioner be able to determine where the person is at the present time, how the person got there, and where the person wants to be in the future. That assessment will be guided by the practitioner's theoretical orientation and, in part, derived by utilizing the Family Wellness assessment questions presented in the previous section. It is vital that the mental health professional be able to identify which of the four quadrants describes an individual's sense of self: no sense of self, poor sense of self, good sense of self, and inflated sense of self.

Case formulations or treatment plans come in a variety of packages. For example, in the cyclical maladaptive pattern suggested by Schacht, Binder, and Strupp (1984) and adapted by Levenson (1995) for dealing with TimeLimited Dynamic Psychotherapy patients, therapists rely on five factors to find a focus for treatment: acts of the self, patients' expectations of others' reactions, acts of others toward the self, acts of self toward the self, and countertransference reactions. Goals are established from these five factors in two areas: new experience and new understanding. Such an organizational system is easy to learn and practice and can be very useful. Other formats exist for how to organize a treatment plan. Ultimately, you (or your agency) will determine which form and style of the treatment plan will be most helpful. This chapter gives you some ideas on how the Family Wellness practitioner develops a treatment plan regarding an individual's sense of self.

While the historic medical model for treatment planning focuses on deficits and needs, the Family Wellness model focuses on strengths and abilities. The intent is not to overlook the needs or problems. In fact, these factors are critical for a complete assessment of a person and the development of a useful treatment plan. The Family Wellness model proposes, "What we focus on grows." That understanding of learning and behavioral theory asserts that the therapist can choose to focus on strengths just as easily as deficits. Family Wellness is a strength-based model. The better choice is seen as focusing on an individual's strengths while recognizing the deficits. The idea is to put deficits into proper perspective by viewing them first through the prism of health and well-being as opposed to the concepts of sickness and illness.

Once an individual's strengths and needs are assessed, the topography (hills and valleys) of an individual's life is put into clearer perspective. Looking for strengths allows the clinician to find a variety of strengths more easily. This perspective also allows the clinician to determine where improvement is needed. This affirming perspective allows for the development of a treatment plan constructed on the solid foundation of a person's strengths instead of the unstable sand of deficits.

The concept of SMART goals—specific, measurable, attainable, realistic, and time limited—is helpful in treatment planning. Ultimately, all goals need to have these characteristics if they are going to be part of an effective treatment plan.

The Family Wellness model uses a very clear, straightforward template for developing an effective treatment plan. The primary components of the template include identifying the presenting or primary issue or concern. Once the problem is identified, ascertain what the desired outcome is. In other words, "What will it look like when the problem is solved?" The more specific the treatment goals are, the more likely the solutions will be identifiable. The next question is, "Who is needed to solve this problem or to obtain the desired outcome?" Those people may be asked to participate in some manner in finding solutions. The next step is to brainstorm possible solutions and prioritize solutions to be implemented. Part of the solution development process includes a "who does what by when" process, ensuring that solutions will actually be implemented. After implementation of a possible solution, a review is held to determine whether the process was effective. If so, the individual can celebrate and move on to work on another issue. If the potential solution was not effective, the review can help determine how the proposed solution can be tweaked to give the best possible chance for success. It is also possible to move to a second potential solution and to go through the "who does what by when" process again. Figure 1.2 shows this treatment plan template. Figure 1.3 shows a sample completed treatment plan focusing on an issue related to self-concept.

The following sections explore a variety of goals and treatment plans that are suggested by an individual's sense of self. We will consider the four possible levels of functioning: no sense of self, poor sense of self, good sense of self, and inflated sense of self.

FIGURE 1.2
FAMILY WELLNESS TREATMENT PLAN

- Presenting or primary issue   _____
- Desired outcome   _____
- Who is needed to solve?   _____
- Brainstorm solutions   _____
                                 _____
                                 _____

- Solution to implement   _____
- Who does what by when?   _____
                                 _____
                                 _____

- Date to reevaluate progress   _____
- Alterations to plan   _____

FIGURE 1.3
COMPLETED FAMILY WELLNESS TREATMENT PLAN

- Presenting or primary issue   *Feelings of inadequacy.*
- Desired outcome   *Increase self-confidence enough to ask a girl out for a date.*
- Who is needed to solve?   *Just self and possible date.*
- Brainstorm solutions   *Go to dating Web site.*
  Ask girl out for coffee.
  Go to church singles group.
- Solution to implement   *Will ask girl from church out for coffee this coming Sunday.*
- Who does what by when?   *This Sunday, I will ask Monica, a casual friend from church, out for coffee after the evening service.*
- Date to reevaluate progress   *Will meet with therapist next Thursday for our scheduled appointment.*
- Alterations to plan   *None at this time.*

No Sense of Self

People who are unable to see themselves as autonomous selves create a highly serious and potentially dangerous condition. Such individuals may become self-destructive because of the despair inherent in nothingness. If they can find self only through association with others, they will often idealize others, and others will always disappoint. This failure to satisfy the quest for self-identification will create a vicious cycle of despair that may result in ever-increasing and desperate efforts at finding self.

Whenever a practitioner is working with someone who does not have a solid sense of self, special care must be taken in developing a treatment plan. If part of the treatment plan involves taking away an unhealthy way of attaching to others in order to provide for a sense of self, the client may be left without anything to hang on to. Removing a foundation, no matter how unstable, without replacing it with another structure creates even more instability. Such a state is terrifying and the person might believe that without anything to hold onto, he or she is in danger of complete oblivion or of falling into the abyss of nothingness.

The most obvious element of a treatment plan for a person who does not have a sense of self is to help the individual develop a well-rounded, realistic, and positive sense of self. Such a task is not easy, however. The assumption is that the development of a sense of self occurs at the earliest of ages and forms in response to attachments made with others in infancy and during the first few years of life. Therefore, an individual will have had years of practicing maladaptive behaviors that make up for a lack of a secure or a "good enough" attachment.

It does little good to tell these individuals what their strengths are. They will either kill the message or kill the messenger. When people have no sense of self, they cannot accept positive feedback. They say that the message is wrong or that the messenger is ineffective in discerning the truth, or both. If the positive message manages, against all odds, to get through, these individuals will not be able to accept it without also attaching, in a very unhealthy manner, to the messenger. In other words, they will imbue the messenger with the power to define them. Therefore, they will overidentify with the messenger and will expect perfection from that person. The expectation of another's perfection becomes the clay feet that hold up their sense of self. Others will always disappoint, and that disappointment will result in a sense of hopelessness within the person who has no autonomous sense of self.

Instead of telling individuals what their strengths are and that they have inherent worth, such individuals need to begin to practice positive self-talk. That behavior can only occur if they are guided into focusing on their strengths instead of on their weaknesses. Individuals often need instruction on affirming introspection. They need to be instructed to withhold self-judgment and focus on their own strengths via methods such as positive self-talk, journaling, and self-affirmations. At the beginning of such work, individuals may frequently need to be reminded that they have to "fake it" until they "make it." They have to make positive statements about themselves even though they do not believe them.

Without a good understanding of self, individuals will be existentially isolated and lonely, no matter how many people are in their lives. A number of interventions and subgoals suggest themselves. One way of discovering self is to become introspective. Achieving that goal involves a journaling process focusing on an individual's sense of self. For example, the client can be instructed to write about aspects of relationships that are fulfilling, frustrating, or untenable. Understanding self in relationship to others helps people understand and value themselves more. The person with no sense of self needs to understand self as autonomous and differentiated from others. The client can be told to write affirmations about self.

This process of writing may provide the individual with a positive sense of self in relationship with others. It can also provide the individual with some insight about himself and about how he relates to others.

The process of helping an individual develop a solid sense of self from nothing is a long-term project. It is generally understood in the psychotherapeutic world that achieving change in the personality is among the most difficult tasks in the profession. How much more difficult is it to actually help an individual construct the personality? One would not expect dramatic personality change in a few short psychotherapy sessions and certainly not in a few psychoeducational classes. An individual with this type of challenge is best served by involvement in long-term, in-depth psychological treatment. Therapists who only do brief therapy should make a referral to someone who is able to invest in long-term work. If you are the person to whom this individual has been referred, then long-term work awaits you. Think of this work as helping the individual in developing the building blocks of self. The apt metaphor is scaffolding, where one task is built or achieved, which then forms the foundation for the next task. This process is repeated until the edifice is erected. Patience on the part of the therapist is mandatory. This type of fundamental change occurs slowly.

Poor Sense of Self

A negative stance toward the self sets the stage for depression, anxiety, and poor choices. People with a poor sense of self often compensate for their perceived inadequacies either by avoiding social interaction altogether (isolating), by doing whatever they deem necessary to obtain the approval of others, or by vociferously demanding agreement from others. Treatment planning for such individuals will depend on which of these behavioral patterns is utilized.

If the individual avoids social contact, the practitioner needs to encourage the client to make contact with others. We know that socialization has huge benefits. Friends are seen as "good medicine" for a variety of problems, including low self-esteem. Friends become a mirror, from which we can see a reflection of who we really are in the present, including our worth and value. Guidano (1991) discusses the "looking-glass effect," wherein our self-knowledge is broadened primarily through our interactions with others. Because of the primacy of obtaining new information about ourselves that can contradict the old, negative self-statements, treatment plans for these individuals need to focus heavily on the development of social interactions, including the development of friendships, involvement in social activities, and participation in team sports.

People with a poor sense of self often have poor social skills. They have not had good experiences with people, either because of personality issues or simply because they have had difficult or traumatic interactions with others. They may not know how to behave socially or how to interact appropriately with others. These people need social skills development classes, psychotherapy groups, or other opportunities to practice and improve their skills. A therapist can develop such classes or groups or can refer individuals with low self-esteem to these types of professional or peer-led groups. Sometimes, other types of groups can be very effective, including specific interest groups such as those organized around scrapbooking, bicycling, computers, photography, and so on.

Groups provide many therapeutic factors (Yalom & Leszcz, 2005) that allow for growth through interaction with others. For example, groups allow individuals to realize that they are not the only ones with certain kinds of problems, that they are not alone. Individuals recognize that they have something of value to contribute to others, that their experiences and words can be valuable to others. They begin to appreciate that they are able to learn from others in a variety of ways. If individual growth can be achieved by viewing self through the reflection of self in the eyes of others, tremendous potential for growth exists if there are many mirrors. Through groups, individuals can see themselves from the differing perspectives of others' eyes.

Be aware, however, that simply encouraging an individual to attend such groups will be totally insufficient. They may not attend because they have a poor sense of self and are afraid of rejection. Rejection would be yet another confirmation of their low worth and value. What these individuals need is a treatment plan that includes goals for the development of specific, basic social interaction skills, such as what to say after you say "Hello." The skills they need will include how to speak up for themselves, how to listen to others, and how to solve problems together. Once people have some basic training in these areas, they can then be referred to groups where they can practice their skills. With this practice, individuals can then generalize those skills into their real lives with much greater efficacy. Thus, an upward spiral for social interaction is developed.

People with low self-esteem often have not had great success in social interactions. They have withdrawn from involvement in most forms of social interaction because they do not wish to put themselves in situations where they will be rejected. The fear of rejection often produces behaviors that invite rejection. This outcome leads to a renewed commitment to the safety of isolation. This pattern, although somewhat effective in preventing new rejection, becomes entrenched as a lifestyle. Once fixed, change is hard to effect. Treatment plans, therefore, need to take into account this tendency to avoid change. People need to be encouraged to try new behaviors even when they do not want to. As previously mentioned, this course of action is called "fake it 'til you make it." The encouragement comes from providing support for individuals through skills development in the therapy office and through in vivo experiences in the community.

Good Sense of Self

Having a realistic and positive sense of self occurs when our subjective self-esteem is aligned with objective reality. This state of consciousness is an ideal, balanced way of living. Although individuals with this way of thinking about themselves have to deal with the same issues that befall all of us, they have an important foundation upon which to live their lives and will likely be able to solve many of the problems that they encounter. When they encounter problems that they cannot solve, they have enough self-confidence to ask for outside help.

Individuals who feel good about themselves, whose foundation for a good sense of self is grounded in reality, do not generally come in for treatment. They have an adequate number of friends, are comfortable "in their own skin," and, in general, for them, "life is good."

Occasionally, an individual with a good sense of self will find his or her way to the therapist's office, generally because the person wants something better or is making an important life decision. Outside professional assistance is desired and valued in formulating or enacting that decision. For example, the person may be making decisions about education or vocational development and seeks outside help with the process. Sometimes people come for treatment because they are connected to someone else who requires professional assistance.

Individuals who have a good sense of self still require affirmation of the strength of their commitment to personal growth and development. Their positive qualities need to be reinforced to help them appreciate how much they have achieved and to acknowledge the success that they have already attained. They need to appreciate themselves and recognize why it is likely that they will be able to reach whatever goals they set before themselves. Treatment plans can be developed that pertain to their current decisions and future goals, which is likely why they sought out treatment in the first place.

People with a good sense of self may also show up to help another person. Such people often attract, and are attracted to, other people with a good sense of self. Even in these situations where healthy people have healthy supports, they sometimes require outside assistance. Occasionally, an individual's equilibrium may be temporarily upset due to significant life changes, such as the death of a friend or family member or making the choice to marry. In these situations, the individual had adequate resources to meet needs in the past. The person now has increased need and inadequate resources. Another possibility is that the person experiences stress because of decreased resources to meet existing needs, such as the development of health problems or a loss of employment. In all of these situations, an otherwise emotionally healthy person may develop anxiety, feel stressed, and seek outside help. This is the healthy response of a healthy person.

Treatment plans with relatively healthy individuals will likely focus on targeted goals brought in by the individual. Sometimes, the person will need help in focusing on the specifics of what they desire. The emotionally healthy person will likely already have most of the resources they need to achieve their goals. Treatment with these individuals will likely be short term and focused.

Inflated Sense of Self

An exaggerated positive sense of self may lead to entitlement issues, maltreatment of others, condescension, and interpersonal difficulties. Some people have an unrealistically high appraisal of themselves. Sometimes this inflated sense of self emanates from specific areas of competency or aptitude. Other times the exaggerated positive sense of self is based on feelings of entitlement due to family history, socioeconomic status, intellectual functioning or educational background, association with people of high status, ethnic heritage, or some positive attribute resulting from genetic inheritance.

When people believe that they are better than others, that belief establishes an above/below relationship with others. This power imbalance may result in individuals who view themselves as leaders and others as followers. Society generally rewards people who are leaders and others are often willing to follow the leader. People with an inflated sense of self may see themselves as better than others based on their leadership qualities. In reality, being a leader or a follower has nothing to do with personal worth or value. The power differential has to do with function. On the other hand, if an individual has an inflated sense of self and attempts to grab control, that person may be seen as arrogant and may alienate others. Children who believe that they are better than others often develop severe social problems with their peers. Adults who have an inflated sense of self often denigrate others in order to affirm and maintain their overly positive self-appraisal.

Treatment planning with people who think too highly of themselves will be difficult because these individuals may not see the need to alter any aspect of themselves. After all, their self-assessment is that they are pretty close to perfect. Instead, these clients tend to believe that any problem they may experience is someone else's fault. If people do not like them it is because they are jealous.

One potential danger in helping someone who has an inflated self-assessment is that the client will need to acknowledge affinity with those whom he has denigrated and shunned in the past. In that process, the potential exists for inadvertently shifting the individual from excessive self-love all the way to self-loathing, which then becomes counterproductive to healthy functioning. Treatment plans for these individuals need to keep the focus for change on the individual and not on the changes others need to make.

Treatment plans for individuals with excessive self-appreciation need to focus on helping them to find a balance between recognizing their strengths and acknowledging that they have deficits as well. These deficits, while not desirable, do not have to be devastating to self-esteem. Individuals must be helped to recognize that personal deficits can be viewed as challenges that can be ameliorated by using the strengths that they already possess.

Summary

Treatment planning is the process of working together with the client to determine the desired outcomes of a course of psychotherapy. It is the establishment of goals that are specific, measurable, attainable, reasonable, and time limited. This process needs to be a mutually shared effort for optimal results. The more focused the treatment plan, the better the prognosis for positive outcomes.

Developing treatment plans for changing an individual's sense of self requires special care to accurately assess the client's current self-appraisal. How individuals think about themselves will reveal much about the resources they have to work with to make whatever changes are desired. To help people make these changes may be challenging but it can also be highly rewarding. An effective treatment plan becomes the road map for change by suggesting practical interventions for achieving goals and arriving at the destination.

INTERVENTIONS

The ultimate outcome of a good assessment and the resulting treatment plan is a set of interventions that can be implemented to produce the desired outcomes in the lives of individuals. Ideally, these interventions are not just things that the practitioner does to an individual but are, instead, a collection of skills that the client or family can practice independent of the practitioner. As our clients improve, via practice, they need the therapist less. Excellent therapists strive to work themselves out of a job with the clients whom we serve.

The implementation of a treatment plan involves utilization of very specific interventions directed at effecting the change that the client desires. Naturally, the interventions are mediated by both an accurate understanding of the individual, the family, and the situation (the assessment) and the development of a specific treatment plan (the set of desired outcomes) that will address the needs of the case.

Helping people focus on who they are and helping them to assert their individuality to become the best they can be is a gift both to our clients and to all of the people in their universe. As people get psychologically healthier they tend to be happier and to become more productive members of society. Being useful to people who desire to achieve their goals is one of the innate satisfactions of this profession.

The first component of any successful intervention is knowledge. With knowledge comes power. As with any change (which is what a treatment intervention is designed for), awareness that something is not working is an important first step. People often recognize that something in their lives is not working when they notice that they are doing things that they wish they would not do and are not doing things that they wish they could do. After noticing a maladaptive aspect of self, people often seek something better. The awareness that a change is needed is good, but it is not sufficient to effect change. Many people are aware that how they are, or what they are doing, is not good for them but they seem unable to change. Insight alone never cured anyone.

The second component of any effective intervention for change is the desire to change. Desire is the decision or choice to change. It is an act of the will. Even the desire for change is insufficient, in and of itself. People do not change simply because they choose to do so. That reality is evident as we think about New Year's resolutions. Within a few days into the new year, the things that we resolved to do are discarded by the wayside while we are still doing things we vowed to quit, often with great gusto.

The third component for change is actual behavioral change, which occurs when people implement a behavioral or attitudinal intervention. Until people actually change a behavior, they may have grown in knowledge or resolve to change but they have not changed. It is a momentous occasion when individuals throw off the shackles of familiar patterns of behavior and courageously step out on a limb to do something differently.

The challenge for the mental health professional is to help an individual see the value in making the proposed change and providing practical interventions that will have the desired outcome. Sometimes the desired outcomes (goals for therapy) are what the individual presents as the reasons for seeking help. Other times, the goals for therapy become clearer as the individual continues in treatment. The treatment plan is mutually developed through careful questioning and a thorough assessment. It may be amended as new information is developed. No matter how the goals are derived, clients may have dramatic qualms about changing the way they have been for much of their lives. Clients, consciously or subconsciously, make cost/benefit analyses to determine if they are willing to risk changing. In these situations, it is important for the therapist to help individuals answer the question, "What's in it for me?" The answer to that question, in part, will depend on how clients assess who they are. If they are in sufficient distress and see the potential value in an intervention, they are more likely to change.

Each of the four possible states of being needs specific interventions, detailed in the sections that follow.

No Sense of Self

The best interventions involve assignments or actions wherein individuals learn and practice new skills that help them think more correctly and feel more deeply about the topic under consideration. The concept of self or self-esteem is nebulous, open to interpretation, ephemeral, and likely unknown to individuals who do not recognize themselves as separate entities apart from important people in their lives. They often think of themselves as having no independent worth or value.

An important goal for a person who does not have a sense of self is to develop a well-rounded, realistic, and positive sense of self. One way a therapist can help such clients develop a sense of self is to help them recognize what they already do well. A question often posed is, "What are three things you do well?" Clients may struggle to come up with even one thing that they do well. These individuals will require a great deal of encouragement to find answers.

Many people believe that it is inappropriate to talk about what they do well. They often say that the answer to that question would be up to someone else. These individuals may, indeed, have a sense of self and therefore fit into one of the other three categories. But some may not; they may be seeking external affirmation.

When an individual is able to state that he does something well, the mere act of making a statement begins to form the basis for identifying himself as a separate entity and for learning how to improve in other areas of life. The person begins to recognize that he has a legitimate reason for believing in himself as a separate and valuable entity within the family or within society as a whole.

Journaling, the homework assignment wherein a person writes about aspects of relationships that are fulfilling, frustrating, or untenable, can help an individual understand herself as separate from others. The individual is directed to write affirmations about the self. Writing positive self-affirmations can provide the individual with a positive sense of self in relationship to others. It may also provide clients with some insight about themselves and about how they relate to others.

Interacting well with those around us requires that we have a strong sense of self. We need to speak up for ourselves, listen to others, and find solutions that work. These are the basic Family Wellness skills that all individuals need to practice in some sort of balance in order to be healthy.

Individuals without a belief in themselves often have trouble speaking up for themselves, listening to others, and cooperatively finding solutions. Therefore, developing a clear appreciation of ourselves as individuals can serve as the foundation for future personal and interpersonal growth.

Assignments that require individuals to assert themselves can be useful in the development of a sense of self. Make sure that all assignments are clear and specific (SMART). One example is to instruct a client to speak up when he or she disagrees with another, knowing that speaking up will likely create discomfort. Individuals have to practice being separate and not simply remaining passive in social environments. Such practice supports the concept of the client as a distinct individual with certain beliefs and values.

Helping an individual to develop a solid sense of self is a long-term project, especially if the starting point is a perceived relative absence of self, a vacuum. One would not expect dramatic personality change in a few short psychotherapy sessions or psychoeducational classes. Nevertheless, practical interventions focused on helping people learn to value self can go a long way in helping them to become mentally and emotionally healthier.

Developing even a rudimentary understanding of self may take a long time to achieve. The practitioner must be secure in his own understanding of himself in order not to be seduced into thinking that such a client's unrealistically positive appraisal of the therapist is true. Working with individuals who have this particular issue is very demanding. The higher the pedestal the therapist is placed on, the farther the therapist can be thrown to the ground when failing to meet the client's expectations for perfection.

People who truly lack a solid sense of self will sometimes show up in psychiatric hospital settings due to acts of self-harm. Long-term, intensive treatment is often required. Interventions must focus on an incremental process of helping the client to accept self as a separate entity and then to embrace and appreciate that individuality. Encourage clients to talk about themselves, especially describing positive attributes. Help them implement specific goals that they have developed in the treatment plan. Reinforce their successes and help them to refocus and redouble their efforts when they do not succeed. Whether they succeed in a stated goal or not, the very act of trying is a success. They are active agents of change rather than passive recipients of what others choose for them. Help them, thereby, to see themselves as separate and capable entities.

Poor Sense of Self

People with a poor sense of self often compensate for their perceived in-adequacies by (a) avoiding social interaction, (b) doing things to obtain others' approval, or (c) demanding agreement from others. Effective interventions for individuals with a low sense of self depend on which of these three behavioral patterns is utilized.

AVOIDING INTERACTION

Some individuals avoid social contact to help them deal with their low self-esteem. These people do not socialize, date, or involve themselves in activities that cause them interpersonal anxiety. Some people are content within their isolation due to the diminution of interpersonal anxiety that comes from not interacting with others. Other people are very discontented because they deeply desire social contact yet recoil from the very possibility of socialization.

If an individual avoids social contact, encouragement to socialize will be a predominant intervention. Our assessment of the individual must determine if the lack of social connection is partially due to having poorly developed social skills. It follows that people who do not think well of themselves will often avoid social environments. Further, since they do not socialize much, they often have underdeveloped social skills. Therefore, social skills development interventions may be highly appropriate.

Involvement in psychotherapy groups or social skills development groups or classes are very important options to help such clients identify the social skills they need to develop further and to give them opportunities for practice. These clients will need encouragement to attend groups since, by definition, they have a hard time in social environments. Discussing with them, ahead of time, the potential value of involvement in such groups can prove to be highly beneficial and effective in getting them to attend and participate in group experiences.

SEEKING APPROVAL

For people who do whatever they believe will help others accept them, encouragement to be judicious in what they do for others will be a predominant intervention. Some people attempt to win approval by being overly deferential to the needs of others and excluding their own needs.

FIGURE 6.2
COMPLETED FAMILY WELLNESS TREATMENT PLAN
FOR PARENTAL LEADERSHIP (CONTINUED)

- Date to reevaluate progress

On Thursday evening, the family will meet to provide the reward for compliance. If the rule is broken during the week, the parents and the offending child will meet and the consequences will be implemented.

- Alterations to plan

If the rewards and consequences do not result in compliance, the parents will decide what additional consequences will be implemented. If no amount of rewards and consequences are successful after 1 month, the parents will seek outside help.

The ability of a parent to find balance between the two jobs of being a leader and being a model is the ultimate goal of any treatment planning for parents. Children need each parent to be good at both jobs.

Whatever balance is achieved between being a leader and a model, the parent must remember that those roles need to remain flexible based on the situation, the age or maturity of a child, the needs of the child, and the needs of the parent. Healthy parents need to be firm and clear about their roles yet flexible and elastic in practice. Determining what a particular parent needs is the task of both assessment and treatment planning. Once that has been accomplished, interventions can be implemented to help effect the desired change.

PRACTICAL INTERVENTIONS: WORKING TOGETHER— UNITED WE STAND

Once a treatment plan has been developed, the practitioner identifies specific activities that the client needs to accomplish. Hearing about healthy relationships and learning how to be a better parent can be useful. However, action is required to actually move from awareness of need for change

---

FIGURE 6.3
COMPLETED FAMILY WELLNESS TREATMENT PLAN
FOR PARENTAL MODELING

- Presenting or primary issue   *Parent rarely plays with the children.*
- Desired outcome   *Parent and children will play together at least two times per week for 30-minute periods.*

- Who is needed to solve?   *Self and children.*
- Brainstorm solutions   *Lay aside leadership role of staying in charge.*
                                 Identify one activity each child enjoys playing.
                                 Develop a play schedule.
- Solution to implement   *Parent will establish a schedule based on each child's availability. Parent to commit to spending time with each child. Play activity will last for 30 minutes at least two times per week. Some activities will be individual with each child alone and some will be group activities involving all the children. Children will pick what activity they want to engage in with their parent.*
- Who does what by when?   *Parent and children will have a family meeting to identify a list of activities that children like, that the parent is willing to do, and that would be either fun or meaningful, or both. Parent and children will agree to a schedule of play dates. Parent and children are responsible for being available to participate. If someone is not available for any reason, that person will advise the other of the reason and will reschedule.*
- Date to reevaluate progress   *When all the children have participated with the parent in individual and group activities at least twice, the family will meet again to affirm or modify the list of potential activities.*

FIGURE 6.3
COMPLETED FAMILY WELLNESS TREATMENT PLAN
FOR PARENTAL MODELING (*CONTINUED*)

- Alterations to plan

If the parent notices an inability to enjoy time playing with children, the parent will talk to other parents who do enjoy fun activities with their children to ask what they do for fun. The amount of time may need to be lengthened or shortened after an effort of at least 2 weeks.

---

to actual change. The Family Wellness practitioner finds ways of getting clients to make changes in their way of living so that actual change occurs.

Couples as Partners

A person moves from being Me to being We through a process of commitment to another person in a relationship, determining to work together as equals in this cooperative venture, and staying connected in a variety of ways to achieve a meaningful, enjoyable, long-term intimate relationship with another human being.

COMMIT

No one can make someone commit to another. That is an individual, personal decision. Individuals sometimes come to therapy offices questioning whether they should be in a relationship with a particular other person, whether boyfriend or girlfriend, fiancé, or spouse. This decision cannot and should not be made by anyone other than the people involved in that relationship. Also, remember that such a commitment is a decision that is made on a daily basis by each person in the relationship.

The clinician's job is this situation is simply to maintain the therapeutic stance of concern, acceptance, genuineness, and empathy. The clinician provides a safe environment in which the person can explore whether it is a good idea to begin or continue a relationship with a particular individual. The therapist must avoid providing opinion or commentary on the decision.

One question that may be helpful is, "Over time in relationship with this person, do you feel better about yourself or worse?" If the answer is worse, the follow-up response is, "Tell me what you do to turn that dynamic around so that you can have a realistic and positive sense of self." People who cannot identify what they do to improve the sense of self in the relationship may need help in knowing, saying, and getting what is desired. These clients may not be using the core skills, especially speaking and cooperation.

Another intervention is to ask an individual to make a "top 10" list of characteristics that attracts him or her into romantic relationship. These characteristics will likely include items such as looks, sense of humor, personality, faith, and so on. After discussion of that list, ask the individual to make another top 10 list of characteristics that would keep him or her committed to the relationship for the long haul. The answers will likely include things such as security, trust, kids, and so on. These answers will provide fertile ground for discussing the things that really matter to an individual for remaining committed to a relationship. Through this exercise, some individuals sadly find that their partner does not possess some of the characteristics that they wished for in a partner. On the other hand, clients may determine that their partner has enough of the desired characteristics to motivate them to put more energy into the relationship. In these situations the clinician can assist clients by identifying which of the three core skills need to be utilized more in an effort to strengthen the relationship. Also, some people find that the problem is not with the partner but in their own ambivalence about being in any relationship. In this situation the clinician can be an important person to talk with because speaking aloud about uncertainty can often help clarify thinking and lead toward decision making.

COOPERATE

Healthy couples work together in a cooperative manner while recognizing and appreciating each other's strengths and weaknesses. They exhibit mutual respect. They balance their power differential in a way that makes sense to them, based on family history, cultural background, and personal choices. Neither person grabs power from the other; neither person relinquishes power; and neither person assumes a role that is not mutually agreed upon. Healthy couples find a way to be together that makes sense for them.

When couples do not have an agreed-upon balance of power or do not respect and value each other, they need practice in problem solving. A sculpt (physical placement of people in varying degrees of closeness to and distance from one another or an object, as described in Chapter 2) or role-plays (as described in Chapter 1) can be helpful in understanding what happens when couples do not work together. Lack of cooperation in a couple relationship creates distance, silence, and coldness.

Couples sometimes have difficulty solving problems because one person assumes all the power or one person relinquishes power and defers to the other. A person who assumes total control excels in speaking up but has taken that skill to the bully level. The person needs to practice listening. The Family Wellness practitioner will guide such a person to purposefully listen more. In that process the person will speak less. A client who consistently acquiesces to the needs of others is good at listening and needs to get better at speaking. The clinician can assign that client the task of determining what he or she wants in a given situation and practicing making statements that begin with the word "I." For example, "I would like for us to go to the movies this Friday afternoon to see a movie of my choice." The reticent client may need practice by writing "I" statements and then saying them out loud. The client can practice in the therapy office with the clinician. The goal is to generalize this newly learned skill so that the client can actually make the desired statements to the other person in real life.

The therapist's task in helping individuals and couples to work cooperatively begins by helping each person see the value of the other person. This basic valuing of another is critical and cannot be taught. However, the clinician can give couples activities to do that will support the concept of equal worth, such as deciding where to go for dinner, planning a vacation, and budgeting.

CONNECT

Staying connected with another person involves physical, sexual, emotional, verbal, spiritual, and temporal components. Many couples are so busy that they do not have time for any kind of connection. Others are so discouraged by their history that they do not make efforts at staying connected or at reconnecting. Others do not want to reconnect.

A popular saying in my office is, "Verbal intercourse is next to sexual intercourse." That phrase gets people's attention (especially men). It is true that when people spend time talking and listening to one another, it is natural to want to be close physically. Expressions of connection include touching, kissing, and embracing. Those behaviors are more likely to occur between couples when they take, and make, time to be together. The chances of connective behaviors occurring increase incrementally when couples talk to one another.

Ask couples to write down what they can do to stay connected if they have "little time, little money, and little kids." They can first write their responses on separate pieces of paper. When they are done, they can compare their ideas. They can then write down the best ideas from both lists. Then, ask the couple to do one of those things on their list in each of the next several weeks. This exercise can prove to be very useful in helping couples to stay connected.

Another idea for couples learning to work together and to appreciate each other is to ask them to make a list of the chores that they generally complete and a list of the chores that their partner usually does. The lists should include chores performed both inside and outside the house. The couple is then asked to identify one chore on the list of what the partner usually does that they are willing to do from time to time. Examples may include washing dishes, changing the oil in the car, and mowing the lawn. Ask couples to tell each other what they are willing to do that their partner normally does. Ask the couple to complete the role reversal in the following week. This process is known as cross-training and is extremely important in helping couples to stay connected. It is also very important for individuals to cross-train in the event that the partner is no longer around to complete the tasks. For example, I have known women who never wrote a check or never used an ATM machine and became nonfunctional when their husbands died or when they divorced. I have also known men who never learned how to cook and would die of hunger if they could not find a restaurant or fast food.

Therapists help couples to appreciate their equal value and find balance in their power differential by helping them to practice their speaking, listening, and cooperation skills. Clinicians provide opportunities for couples to discuss and demonstrate their commitment to each other, their cooperation, and their connection.

Parents as Leaders

Having children is one way to remain humble. The difficult job of being parents in a healthy family is for each parent to be both a leader and a model. As such, leadership is about accepting the role of being a care provider for the children and providing clear rules, establishing and enforcing rewards and consequences, and staying in charge. Being a model is another aspect of leadership in that the parents purposefully set aside the above relationship in order to play with the children without being in charge of the activities, to encourage children, to learn by listening, and to know each other better by talking together. In this process, the leader as model temporarily assumes a beside or even a below position with the children. That temporary choice allows children to practice their speaking, listening, and cooperation skills and helps them on their way toward adulthood.

The humility aspect of parenthood involves the reality that just when we get good at our job, the children change and we need to adjust what we have been doing. The good news is that we do not have to be perfect as parents, just good enough. We become good enough parents when we learn to be clear yet flexible when dealing with hierarchy, family roles, and boundaries within the family.

HIERARCHY

Parents need to be in charge in order to provide adequate structure for their families. Parents often seek outside help when they feel powerless in their role as parents. Children of every age often make decisions that run counter to parental wishes or rules. When children do not have parents who remain in charge, they will often make very bad decisions.

A parent who does not know how to stay in charge may need education in how to make rules that are clear and specific. The parent may also need assistance in learning to stick together with the spouse, partner, or other adults. A third issue may be difficulty in enforcing rewards and consequences. Generally children learn best by the consistent enforcing of rewards and consequences.

Help parents know exactly what behaviors they desire from their children. Help them to be clear in expressing their expectations to their children. Help them to be consistent in the application of consequences appropriate to the behavior exhibited by their children.

In the therapy office, parents can practice identifying their values, the rules that attach to those values, and the positive rewards that they are willing to give for compliance and the negative consequences that they will consistently enforce for noncompliance. Parents can be asked to write these items down, can talk to the therapist about them, or can talk to each other about what they believe, what they want, and what they are willing to do to get compliance. This process can be helpful not only in parenting but also in the solidification of the couple relationship. This process can also sometimes work with divorced co-parents.

The therapist can demonstrate the importance of enforcing rules by having a client push against the partner or the therapist until the partner moves backward. This sculpt demonstrates that children always push against limits. If the child is successful in pushing the limit-setter backward, it signifies that the child is in charge. This is a very scary place to be if you are a child and can do whatever you want. No limits.

The therapist can demonstrate the importance of parents sticking together by having the couple hold hands and stand very close together. The therapist can take on the role of a child and attempt to move the parents away from each other. When the therapist is successful in moving the parents apart, it demonstrates the concept of "divide and conquer." In that situation, parents do not have mutual support and unhealthy triangulation occurs, two against one. When the therapist cannot move the parents, the parents are showing that they are united on behalf of the children. Together, they are much stronger than alone and the children benefit from that demonstration of hierarchy.

FAMILY ROLES

The needs for security, safety, expression, and belonging are best met when each person of a family understands and does their role well. Parents are in charge, in the above role. They take care of the children. Children are taken care of, in the below role. Siblings are in a beside role with one another. Adults are in the beside role, working together as equals.

Some children do not want to obey their parents. In fact, they want to be in charge of themselves and of their parents. In those situations, the parents need to speak up more and enforce appropriate consequences that will encourage the child to comply with parental demands. Parents need to be careful to also play with, encourage, and listen to their children. When parents create a playful, caring environment at home, the children will more easily choose to comply and embrace their role as children. As children grow older, the parents need to be flexible regarding rules so that children have more practice making their own decisions and choosing from an ever-expanding array of options. In so doing, children will practice making adult decisions while in the safety of the home environment.

The clinician can work with adults to strengthen their role as parents while simultaneously working with children to help them utilize their skills for changing family rules. The clinician can ask children, in child or family therapy situations, which rules are useful within the family and can then ask if there are any rules they would like to change. When they offer several ideas, ask them to pick one. When children ask for several changes at the same time they are likely not to get anything from the parents. Review with children the concepts that parents are in charge and that children are asking for a change by stating what they want, being willing to listen to the parents, looking for areas of agreement, stating what they are willing to do in order to get what they want, offering trades and compromises, and then accepting whatever the parent decides. Finally, children are directed to thank parents for listening to them, even if the answer was no.

When adults or couples understand their role, when children understand and accept their role, and when siblings work and play together, the entire family functions in a more organized manner.

BOUNDARIES

Boundaries are the underlying family rules that express who is allowed to do what with whom and when. Boundaries are mostly related to dyadic relationships between any two people in a family. The norms of a family are established by the adults. Once norms are made, they are difficult to change. Nevertheless, changes are appropriate in given circumstances, such as when someone becomes ill, when someone loses a job, when there is protracted absence of any member, and so on.

Clients with boundary issues can be relatively easy to recognize and change, such as when a child feels neglected by a parent, feels picked on by a sibling, or is inseparable from another family member. These situations can be identified and corrected by looking at the skill that is used and what skills need to be used more or less, and by getting the individuals to make the necessary changes. A father can spend more time with a child, or siblings can be encouraged to find solutions on their own, or children can be encouraged to identify activities they can do separately from other siblings.

Some clients have significant boundary issues with severe societal and legal ramifications, such as when a parent engages in inappropriate physical or sexual contact with children. These situations are extreme and will require expert treatment and understanding of how and why the boundaries were crossed.

Alejandra became very ill from a chronic pain condition. She also became depressed and ceased doing chores and fulfilling other household functions. As a result of her pain and difficulties with sleep, Alejandra moved into an extra bedroom. Her husband asked their oldest daughter, Maria, to do more work around the house to pick up the slack left by Alejandra's condition. Soon Maria was vacuuming, doing the wash, cooking, and caring for the younger children. After a period of time, Maria was asked to sleep in her father's bedroom. Ultimately, Maria was violated sexually, her father was sent to jail, her mother attempted suicide, and the children were temporarily placed with other relatives.

Clear violations of societal norms can have severe implications for all involved, such as the case of Maria. Other violations are annoying but can be easily corrected. The therapist can help families by having a clear understanding of the dyadic relationships within the family. Children can be asked to draw pictures of the family and the therapist can identify relative closeness and distance of family members as well as noticing any family members that are missing from such drawings. Therapists can then make interventions that allow people to practice connection or distance, as indicated by what they need to find balance. Examples of activities that promote closeness include directing each parent to spend time with each child. Moms can go shopping with the children separately to let them know that each is special. Dads can spend time with their sons and daughters doing activities the kids enjoy. Moms sometimes allow a son to drive to the store. Spouses go out on dates without the children. Siblings are encouraged to do things together and apart.

Families that respect the boundaries in the various dyadic relationships function better. The therapist seeks to identify which relationships are functioning well and encourages continued connection and distance. The therapist is also aware of boundaries that are enmeshed and need increased separation as well as boundaries that are so distant that connection must be encouraged. When couples and other dyads within a family work well and in a balanced way, the family becomes more united. Such a family is healthy, safe, and fun.

SUMMARY

The ability to build a strong family begins with the construction of a strong enough foundation that encourages each individual to speak, listen, and cooperate. When healthy individuals commit to another, they choose to be together and they also choose how they will be with one another. If they have children, they now become parents who realize that families work best when the parents are in charge, when there is room for everyone to be close and to be apart, and when the concept of change is not only expected, it is embraced as part of the cycle of life. Sometimes a single parent needs to use the speaking, listening, and cooperation skills even more because the job of being a parent is very demanding and requires as many resources and supports as possible.

The role of the psychotherapist who utilizes the Family Wellness model is to help families construct or remodel the individual or familial home. The therapist assumes that the house has "good bones" and therefore looks for areas of strength while not overlooking areas of potential danger. Certain aspects of personality may need to be constructed while other areas of functioning may simply need to be remodeled or strengthened. The goal of treatment becomes helping individuals and families construct their own home, with their own personalities, so that they can take pride in, and take ownership of, having constructed a beautiful place to belong and a safe place to grow.

7

Room to Be Close and Apart

Me and You

HEALTHY COUPLES AND families make room, within their relationships, for each person to be close to and apart from each other, thereby maintaining both their connectedness and their individuality. The clinician who utilizes the Family Wellness model seeks to find the balance between connection and separation that fits the specific members of that relationship. These competing needs are dynamic rather than static and are based on the personalities of the couple or family, on the cultural backdrop of each person, and on the agreed-upon norms for their relationship.

Theories of human development and attachment often begin at birth. For example, Erickson's model of the psychosocial stages of development begins with the oral-sensory stage, where the major task is basic trust versus mistrust (Erickson, 1963). We know, however, that much of who we become begins in the womb. Some theories posit human social development as beginning prior to birth, in the prenatal stage (Newman & Newman, 1999).

John Bowlby (1988) described attachment, which can be seen as the capacity to be close to and apart from others, as a behaviorally organized pattern of infant signals and adult/parent responses that lead to a protective, trusting relationship. He believed that this dynamic occurred in the earliest stage of development.

Ainsworth (1973, 1985) wrote about five stages in the development of attachment, beginning from birth to 3 months, wherein the infant engages in certain behaviors (including sucking, rooting, grasping, smiling, cuddling, and visual tracking) to maintain closeness with the caregiver. According to Ainsworth, as infants progress through these stages they are more responsive to familiar figures than to strangers, seek physical proximity and contact with objects of attachment, form internal mental representations of the object of attachment, and use a variety of behaviors to influence the behavior of the objects of attachment.

Whereas we usually think of infants as being delicate and totally dependent on care providers for their survival, we have learned that infants actually exert a great deal of influence over adults through their behavior. Infants choose to have guardians approach them when they have certain needs, such as to be fed, to be changed, or to be held. Infants also choose when they want to be left alone, such as when they want to explore, sleep, or simply be content.

Adults engage in similar behaviors of attaching to others and being distant from others. The Family Wellness model posits that even in a committed relationship, individuals need room to be close and room to be apart. Adults need skills to connect with others in meaningful ways that can be mutually beneficial. Adults also need skills to seek space and allow distance from important people in their lives. If adults require others to be with them at all times, therapists deem these relationships to be enmeshed or codependent. If adults live their lives so independently that they do not need others, their relationships may be considered similar to a roommate arrangement or a business partnership. Healthy couples and families find a balance between being together and being apart.

Some people believe that if they are too close to others, they may lose their individuality, their identity. Some people are so afraid of losing themselves that they never open up to others and invite intimacy. These individuals may become relationship averse because of fears of personal annihilation. They become fervently self-sufficient and make little effort at interconnection. On the other hand, some individuals desperately seek connection but do not have the skills necessary to form lasting committed relationships. These individuals are willing to lose their identity in order to form a connection.

The Family Wellness model seeks to help individuals find a balance between being rugged individualists and being completely consumed by another. In the context of a committed couple relationship and within a family, the Wellness practitioner helps individuals find both intimacy and distance, without losing either individuality or connection.

ASSESSMENT: "I'M ALONE, YOU'RE ALONE— LET'S BE ALONE TOGETHER"

Human beings have two basic jobs: to be individuals and to connect with others. Within the couple and family, healthy individuals are able to balance these two jobs in a way that works well for both the individual and the couple or family. The healthy person has the ability to know how to be close without losing a sense of self and how to be apart without becoming disconnected. The assessment of an individual's ability to juggle these apparently competing demands will help the therapist in identifying the client's treatment needs and suggest interventions to produce the desired outcomes.

Closeness produces intimacy. Closeness is what keeps existential abject loneliness at bay. Some people have been hurt by prior ventures into closeness. They never allow themselves to truly know another person and never allow themselves to be known by others. It is a delicate balance to know and to be known. This capacity for intimacy is calibrated by the story of our lives. If we have been hurt in the past when we sought out intimacy, we will be shy about opening ourselves up to be hurt again. The pain caused by efforts at connection can come from rejection and abandonment as well as from engulfment and control. Either result of being devalued or appropriated as a commodity by another can produce a fear of connection. By listening to an individual's thoughts and feelings about the meaning of intimacy and connection, the clinician can determine whether the individual has previously made efforts at connection and what the results of such efforts have been.

The mental health professional can evaluate an individual's capacity for intimacy by asking about his or her ability to trust and risk, two significant aspects of connection. Since intimacy requires both trust and risk, we need to understand these personal characteristics that have interpersonal implications.

Trust is defined by *Webster's* as a "reliance on the integrity, strength, ability, surety, etc., of a person or thing; confidence." In order to develop a sense of trust in another, one must be willing and able to observe another's actions and determine the inner workings that result in the external deeds. To do that requires a degree of social intelligence, combined with a willingness to ascribe meaning to nuance of attitude and action. We make these judgments many times in our relationships with others. To the degree that we are competent in making these judgments, we increase our capacity to make sound determinations of the trustworthiness of another. Trust requires that individuals have a history with each other that has produced positive results in a variety of settings and experiences. The more positive outcomes result from efforts at connection, the more we can trust the other person to be trustworthy.

Risk is defined by *Webster's* as "exposure to the chance of injury or loss; a hazard or dangerous chance." Risk is normally defined by the potential for loss. It can also be defined by the potential for gain, as in "I risked everything for love." That possible gain, however, is offset by the dangerous aspect of potential loss. Therefore, many people make risk assessments regarding their relationships; they make cost-benefit analyses. They weigh the chance for negative outcomes against the value of possible positive outcomes to determine if they are willing to engage in deeper levels of intimacy. To the degree that individuals remain in a self-protective mode that values preservation of self above potential for connection, they will not risk. When the need or desire for connection exceeds their fears, they will chance intimacy. The therapist must listen closely to an individual's cost-benefit analysis to ascertain whether the person is willing to risk.

While a complete formal assessment of an individual's capacity for intimacy can become a very complicated process of history taking, gathering information from other sources, the use of testing instruments, and so on, many mental health professionals are in situations that require almost instantaneous assessments and judgments about an individual's placement on an imaginary continuum of intimacy. In those situations, the clinician should evaluate the individual's capacity for trust and risk within a given relationship to assess how close and how distant the individual is. Having determined that placement, the clinician can then work with the client to choose desired outcomes for treatment.

Some people may have severe psychological problems that result in significant difficulties in connection. They may consistently refuse to let others know who they are. They will not answer direct questions and will reveal very little about themselves. Diagnostically, they may suffer from paranoia or a personality disorder, such as schizoid. The diagnosis of these individuals is outside the scope of this book. Nevertheless, these individuals are sometimes part of the relationships we treat, either as clients or spouses of clients. Clinicians must be aware of the potential for severe difficulties in relationship for some individuals.

In most couple and family relationships, individuals may have crises wherein they find themselves unable to connect with others at an intimate

FIGURE 7.1
THE RELATIONSHIP CYCLE (USED BY PERMISSION OF
FAMILY WELLNESS ASSOCIATES)

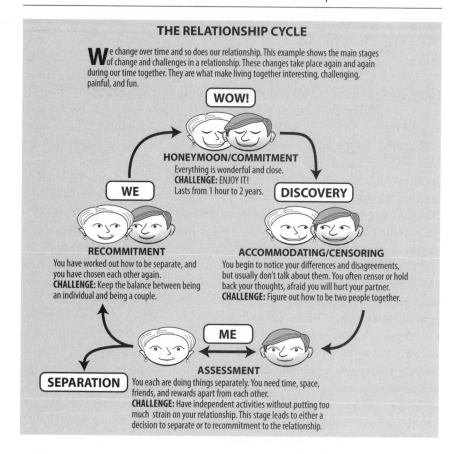

level or wherein they seek extreme distance from one another. This failure to connect or desire to separate can occur at predictable times in the life of a relationship.

The relationship process generally moves from a honeymoon or commitment phase, to an accommodation or censoring phase, to an assessment phase, and finally to a recommitment phase. These four phases of the relationship cycle can be used as an assessment tool to help individuals determine where they are at any point in time in the relationship, where they believe their spouse is, and where they would like to be. Figure 7.1 can be used for assessment, treatment planning, and intervention purposes.

Assessing a relationship, whether a couple or a family, requires the clinician to understand that healthy individuals require closeness and distance within any kind of dyad. Closeness does not have to produce loss of identity; distance does not have to produce loss of connection. Room to be close and room to be apart are essential aspects of a couple or family being able to function well over a protracted period of time.

TREATMENT PLANS: HOW TO BE CLOSE WITHOUT LOSING ME; HOW TO BE DISTANT WITHOUT LOSING US

Individuals with difficult attachment issues need help in finding a balance between connection and isolation. They either seek closeness at all costs because they are deathly afraid of being alone, or they require distance because they fear losing their identity if they get too close to others. Other people may get too close or be too distant for reasons having nothing to do with attachment, such as a job that requires long-distance travel, military deployment, incarceration, excessive activities and commitments, fairy tale ideas about love and romance, lack of other friendships, and severe chronic illness within a couple or family.

The psychosocial crisis of infancy is trust versus mistrust. Trust in this context refers to the predictability, dependability, and genuineness of another person (Rempel et al., 1985). Interpersonal trust grows as a relationship deepens. In the important relationships of life, we take risks. We reveal ourselves and risk rejection. We also risk increased intimacy. The ability to trust someone is not only a statement about us in the current relationship and the nature and depth of the other person; it is also a revelation of our past in context with others. It is a statement about ourselves in relationship with others, past and present. Our capacity to trust predicts our capacity for engaging in intimate connection with others in the future.

> Samantha is a middle-aged female who has been divorced three times. She has two children who live in other states and who have almost no contact with her. Several years ago, Samantha took her mother in because of her mother's need for physical care. Samantha reported, "Mother was cruel, heartless, and just plain mean." Her mother had recently died when Samantha came to my office in an obviously depressed state. She acknowledged that she was relieved that she did not have to care for her mother any longer. Samantha reported that she had no friends and was not sure she had

any particular reason, or desire, to live. She said that nobody really cared about her.

While Samantha was relating the sad state of her interpersonal life, she mentioned that a young woman at work seemed to like her. She said that this woman would call her frequently and ask if she wanted to go out for coffee, a meal, or the movies. Samantha was annoyed by the woman's constant efforts to get her to go out. Samantha said, "I don't really care to have any friends. I don't care about their lives. I don't want to know anything about her or her family!" After making this strong statement, Samantha returned to lamenting her lack of connection with others. She did not appreciate the causal connection between her attitude toward others in her life and the fact of her isolation.

To be truly emotionally healthy, we have to be comfortable with ourselves (having a realistic and positive sense of self). We have to know how to be alone without being lonely. We look for opportunities to attend to things that can enrich us, such as making time for personal interests and hobbies, and taking time to complete chores and other tasks that need to be done or that we choose to do. This comfort with ourselves means that we like ourselves and like to spend time with ourselves. Besides enjoying time alone, we also enjoy connecting with others. Some people have only a few good friends; others have many deep connections. One is not better than the other. The number and depth of friendships is largely determined by personality and the actions individuals demonstrate that show that they desire either time alone or time with others.

Determining whether a particular lifestyle is healthy or not (few friends versus many friends) depends largely on how individuals interpret their condition. Some people can be lonely in a crowd. For other people, two is a crowd. Treatment plans for being close and apart will depend on the assessed needs of the individual client.

The mental health professional can develop a substantive treatment plan to improve the individual's ability to balance time for self and time with others by utilizing the relationship cycle as both an assessment tool and a treatment planning tool.

Wow

A relationship usually begins with getting to know someone enough to fall in love, which starts the Wow stage of a relationship cycle. This process can be instantaneous, as in being hit by Cupid's arrow, or can take a relatively long period of time as friendship gradually blossoms into romance. In either event, the first phase of a relationship is often a honeymoon stage of commitment. This period is characterized by feeling as if you are walking in the clouds, every love song was written just for you, and the word that seems to come out of your mouth most often is "Wow!" This period can be short or long. The challenge is to thoroughly enjoy it. Who doesn't want to be in love?

Treatment planning often revolves around one or both individuals wanting to return to this phase of the relationship. Therefore, interventions will likely involve asking people to remember what this time in their life was like, what each of them did to nurture the Wow state of being, and asking them to again commit to doing those things. Some people never had a Wow phase. They met, they got pregnant or one of them was going off to war, and they committed to each other. In some cases, one or both already had children from prior relationships and so the couple became an instant family. Couples who never had a Wow phase often have a harder time exhibiting a loving, caring relationship. In these situations, the treatment plan will call for each of them to determine exactly what they seek in their relationship, having them be precise about their goals for the relationship, identifying what each is willing to do to achieve the desired outcomes, and having them define mutual goals as a couple.

In the case of adults who have children, the emphasis in treatment planning is to help individuals, whether they be single parents, part of a couple with children, or part of a couple within a stepfamily, to develop closer connections with their romantic partners. In the case of a single parent who is not in a romantic relationship, the emphasis is on learning how to establish and maintain meaningful friendships. Goals need to be specific, as in having a date night once a week, on Thursday evenings at 7:00 p.m., that will last for at least one and a half hours. The more specific the treatment plan, the greater the likelihood of actually achieving the goals of that plan.

Discovery

The Discovery stage of a relationship occurs as the couple is getting to know each other better. At first, most individuals put their best foot forward in an effort to impress the other person. That impression works well enough for the couple to fall in love. Over time, individuals begin to recognize something to which they were mostly blind during the Wow phase, which is that their partner is not perfect. Entering a relationship, individuals already know that they are not perfect. Over time they reveal their imperfections and begin to notice the imperfections in the other. At first, partners attempt to deny the obvious, by accommodating and censoring. They notice their differences and disagreements but usually do not talk about them. They may hold back certain thoughts because they are afraid that they may hurt the other. The challenge during the Discovery stage is to figure out how to be two people together.

Treatment planning for individuals in the Discovery phase of a relationship generally involves having couples overtly establish the norms for their relationship. When couples are not overtly focused on what the norms are within the relationship, very unhealthy patterns can emerge. For example, it may become unacceptable for one or both individuals to state what they want for fear of offending the other. Or the couple may engage in certain behaviors or activities because that is what they have always done, without determining if those activities continue to meet one or both people's needs in the present. Norms are hard to change once they have been established. Therefore, the Discovery stage is a great time to make the covert overt.

Treatment plans will likely include goals that support the importance of both individuals using their speaking, listening, and cooperating skills in the service of determining how they want to be as a couple. Each person has the responsibility of being involved in determining how decisions will be made, by whom, under what circumstances, and how the couple defines itself in terms of power differential and mutual respect. The rules for the relationship must be openly discussed and mutually agreed upon in order for the relationship to be satisfying.

Me

The Me stage of a relationship occurs after the couple has lived together for some time. Over time, individuals begin to engage in the activities that they enjoy or find exciting. Although identified as part of a couple, each person is still an individual. As such, each person needs time, space, friends, and activities that are rewarding apart from each other. Having divergent interests is not the problem. Having only divergent interests can become a major problem. The challenge during this phase of a relationship is for individuals to have independent activities without putting too much strain on the relationship.

Treatment planning for the Me stage often involves helping each individual identify and articulate what they are passionate about while ensuring that the needs of the couple are satisfied. The main rule about separate activities is that those activities cannot undermine the marriage or relationship. In other words, a couple who chooses to date other people is also choosing to no longer be in a relationship. That choice to date others is in direct competition with a basic tenet of most relationships: fidelity. A person who loves playing softball can do so without necessarily endangering the relationship. Nevertheless, some people play so much softball that they forget about the needs of their partner or family. Therefore, something positive can become a negative in a particular relationship.

Often, couples who find themselves in the Me stage are so committed to good things that they pull away from each other. Such activities may include athletics, community responsibilities, friendships, and so on. The activities themselves are not bad. The way they are done, the time required, or the lack of communication within the relationship about those activities may turn something positive into a negative. Treatment plans for people in this phase of a relationship often involve the need for increased communication.

The Me stage can become an extremely dangerous time in the life of a couple. Strong commitment to outside events, interests, and people can cause a great deal of strain within the couple. One or both people's needs may not be met by the other. Couples may become physically distant from one another, they may become emotionally alienated, and they may lose their sexual connection. Sometimes, people seek out other people, things, or rewards to meet their needs. These outside dangers to the life of a relationship may be other people, as in having an affair; other things, as in the use of substances; or other rewards, as in becoming a workaholic. What they are really seeking is the "wow" that was lost, but they have lost hope that they can re-establish it with their partner. These dangers may lead to the potential for separation and divorce. Often people do not realize that they are in this phase of a relationship until it is (almost) too late.

We

When people recognize the potential dangers in being so distant that they have neglected to care for one another, they are in an optimal position to make changes. Individuals within a relationship can choose to recommit to a We stage. This decision comes after awareness of distance and the desire for renewed reconnection. Individuals in this stage of the relationship have figured out how to be separate and how to be close. They have chosen to make the relationship their priority. The challenge in the We stage of a relationship is finding a way to keep the balance between being an individual and being a couple.

Treatment planning for the We phase generally involves affirming that individuals have a right to have separate interests and activities while ensuring that they also share some activities and interests. The different interests keep a marriage hot while the shared activities and values are what hold the marriage together. When people know how to be close and how to be separate, they are able to continue their individual interests and bring those back to the relationship, thereby making the marriage stronger. When both people in a relationship are able to do that, they each appreciate their individuality and treasure their couple relationship. Couples who can successfully maneuver through the We phase have a realistic and positive sense of self and are able to form solid relationships.

What is interesting about the relationship cycle is that people who manage to periodically get back to the We stage often enjoy the Wow stage again and again. As we said, who doesn't want to be in love? This potential for positive change is what makes periodically reviewing the relationship cycle extremely important and useful for assessment, treatment planning, and intervention purposes.

PRACTICAL INTERVENTIONS: CLOSENESS BREEDS INTIMACY; ABSENCE MAKES THE HEART GROW FONDER

After reviewing the relationship cycle with clients, the Family Wellness practitioner is able to help individuals identify which stage in the cycle they are in and where they believe their partner to be. Even a discussion on the similarity or differences of their opinions can yield useful information for how well a couple communicates. A frank discussion of where they are and what they would like for their relationship can be beneficial in the implementation of practical interventions that have a high likelihood of producing positive changes.

Room to Be Close

In order to feel comfortable being close to someone without fearing that he or she will be lost, an individual needs to have a realistic and positive sense of self. Only then will an individual be able to form a solid couple. The intensity of a couple's physical and emotional closeness demonstrates where they are on the relationship cycle. Individuals who cannot bear to be apart and yearn to know everything there is to know about one another are generally in the Wow stage of a relationship. These people are constantly talking to or texting one another. They barely look at the menu when they are in a restaurant because they cannot bear to take their eyes off one another. From the outside, that type of closeness may seem odd. From the inside, that level of connectedness is delicious.

The reason that the Me stage of a relationship can, in the extreme, produce the possibility of separation and divorce is that people in this stage may have lost the closeness that they formerly enjoyed. People who feel distance from one another yearn for closeness and may have lost hope that they can ever find that exquisite connection again. As a result, they look for someone, or something, to reinvigorate them. Unfortunately, whatever the outcome, the new connection is almost always an ephemeral fix.

Couples who yearn for closeness can be invited to identify their hopes, dreams, and interests. They can then share those ideas and look for areas of agreement. Couples can be assigned homework where they pick one thing that they want to do together but have not had the opportunity to do in a long time. They are given the task of actually accomplishing the event between treatment appointments. They should be asked to identify short-, medium-, and long-term goals, so that they can accomplish some things quickly and can look forward to doing things together into the future.

Sometimes, one person wants to do things with the partner but the partner is not very inclined to cooperate. In those situations, the therapist can coach the person who wants change to speak up clearly about that desire. The next task is to listen carefully to what the spouse says. Listening to the words, the underlying emotions, and the energy the spouse displays will reveal a great deal about what the spouse needs. The therapist can then encourage the client to meet the spouse's needs in order to also have a chance to do what the client desires them both to do together. This is the skill of cooperation as shown through the ability to negotiate. It is an overt discussion of each person's needs and what an individual is willing to do to accomplish what is desired. This process is not manipulation, which is a covert effort to effect change by engaging in a discussion while keeping a hidden agenda. That agenda is about getting what one wants without caring about what the spouse wants. In cooperation, the desired outcome is a win-win. I want a good deal for me and I want a good deal for my partner. When I negotiate well, each of us gets what we want.

In a truly healthy relationship with significant levels of closeness and connection, the individuals are able to see themselves for who and what they are: valuable and desirable. These relationships breed intimacy, which results in safety for each person. This kind of couple is like a ship that can withstand many storms, because they have many ties that bind them together.

Room to be close in a relationship is about increased connection. The clinician fosters behaviors in couples that encourage talking, listening, and cooperating about activities that they want to do together. When individuals are getting their needs met within the relationship, they are able to focus on separate activities that they desire. They can then engage in these separate activities without causing stress on the relationship. In fact, healthy couples who know how to be close also enjoy time apart, which only serves to make their connection stronger because of the new energy they continuously bring back to their relationship.

Room to Be Apart

A healthy couple can only support being apart if they know how to be close. On the other hand, some members of a couple are very distant. They desire to be apart often and seldom desire connection. These individuals are likely in the Me stage of a relationship. They have moved further and further apart as they have found activities that consume their lives. They have forgotten why the couple came together in the first place. These individuals are living parallel lives, like roommates, functioning more or less adequately and taking care of business. However, they have lost their emotional connection. Some people go so deeply into the Me stage of a relationship that they separate and divorce. If the commitment to divorce is absolute, they will not likely come to the therapy office. Even when they do, it may be simply to be able to say that they tried everything but the marriage did not work.

Many people who come to therapy are individuals who want increased distance from their partner yet want to maintain the relationship. They may not know how to accomplish this desired goal and need instruction in speaking up for their needs. They may also have to learn to cooperate, that is, to take care of their spouse's needs so that they have a better chance of getting their own needs met. Some individuals do not believe that it is possible or appropriate to do many activities apart from one another and still maintain a healthy relationship. These individuals need instruction in finding the balance between time for self and time for each other.

Determining in which relationship stage individuals find themselves and what they desire for themselves and for their partner requires focused interventions to help people achieve their goal of more room to be apart. The therapist can assist such couples by asking them to identify and then discuss activities about which they are passionate and which they would like to do separately from their spouse. Such discussions will likely yield much information about how each person views the couple dyad, including their values about themselves and what it means to be in relationship. The therapist can use that information in helping them find common ground so that their need for individual time can be balanced with their need for connection.

When individuals have sufficient time alone to do things that enrich them, they often desire to share their experiences with their partner, which produces more time together. In order to be able to be both alone and together, individuals need to have a strong sense of self and have excellent skills for connection.

SUMMARY

The ability to attach and detach in a healthy relationship requires two individuals that are healthy in their sense of self and in their ability to connect with others. The Family Wellness model identifies these as the two jobs of the individual. Most therapists agree that humans develop their sense of self in the earliest years based on the primary relationship within the family. Harry Stack Sullivan wrote, "The self may be said to be made up of reflected appraisals" (Mullahy, 1952, p. 22). Object relations and attachment theories teach us about children's elastic connection between themselves, their need for safety, and their need for exploration. Adults also appear to have a strong need for individuality and an equally strong need for connection.

Meeting the dual needs for room to be close and room to be apart in a relationship is the subject of many appointments in a therapist's office. Having a model such as the relationship cycle can assist both clinicians and clients in determining where they are and where they want to be in their relationship.

8

Expect Change

The Only Constant in Life

If you always do what you've always done, you'll always get what you've always gotten. If you want something different, you've got to do something differently.

Anonymous

HEALTHY INDIVIDUALS RECOGNIZE and embrace change as an important aspect of life and growth. They learn to deal with expected changes so that they can handle the unexpected changes that may come into their lives.

Psychosocial theory confirms what we already know: Change is hard. People get used to being a certain way and dancing a certain dance. Over time, those patterns become ruts. Some ruts become extremely difficult to change due to the activation of neural pathways toward pleasure and due to physiological and psychological addictions. At times we become aware that a change is necessary, and we may even make a commitment to change, yet we stop short of change. Few people change simply because of insight. People can know the terrible effects of certain chemicals yet ingest them anyway. Insight alone never cured anyone. The decision to change, an act of the will, is good but is also insufficient. Insight and a decision to change must be supported by new behaviors to actually effect change. Even then, the temptation is to return to the older, deeper ruts of behavior upon meeting any obstacles or stress.

190

Randy vehemently swore that he was not an alcoholic. He said he knew this because he could stop drinking anytime he wanted. In fact, he proudly announced, he had stopped drinking many times this past year. According to Randy, his wife had coerced him into coming to therapy and he was only in my office to please her and get her off his back. This course of counseling was not likely to be successful because Randy did not believe he had a problem, did not want to be in my office, and had only come because of his wife. As a result, he had no insight, had made no decision to change, and did not plan on making any behavioral changes.

I asked Randy how long he thought he could go without drinking alcohol. I suggested that, since he had no drinking problem, he might be able to abstain from drinking for a month. He countered that he would prove to me that he had no problem by not drinking for three months. About one and a half weeks later, Randy called and sheepishly asked for an appointment. He had been stopped by the police while driving drunk. He was now ready to work on his problems.

The Family Wellness model asserts that when an individual has sufficient resources to meet his needs, he will likely live stress free, at least in the arena being considered. This includes the very important arenas of finances, time, energy, health, relationships, and so on. When changes occur in the balance of resources and needs, however, stress develops. Two possibilities may change the balance: An individual's resources may diminish or that person's needs may increase. Either of these events creates stress. Often, both of these events occur at the same time: Resources diminish and needs increase.

The good news is that stress is the signal that a change is necessary. When individuals pay attention to that signal, they are in an optimal position to make the changes required to find a new balance in life. They may seek out additional resources to help achieve the new equilibrium, which may replenish spent resources or may strengthen the foundation when additional needs have been piled on. Sometimes a person needs to diminish the need, if at all possible.

People can obtain additional resources or diminish needs by using the three core skills that are the hallmark of the Family Wellness model. They can speak up to a boss, a friend, or a family member to either decrease need or increase resources. Healthy individuals can listen to the same others in an effort to more clearly understand the issues and then take actions that will ameliorate the situation. In the worst-case scenario, a person may come to understand that the difficult situation will not change and that a bad situation must be accepted. In that case, the individual must adapt to the new reality.

> Richard was an extremely hard-working painter. One day, the scaffolding he was on collapsed and he fell to the ground. He injured his left shoulder and lower back. Subsequently, Richard developed a chronic pain condition in his shoulder and back, with sciatica that ran down both legs. He was unable to work. His income dropped dramatically. He lost his house and a car, and his marriage almost ended because he was constantly irritable and because his libidinal interests almost entirely vanished. He was extremely depressed about the past and anxious about the future. Psychotherapy helped Richard accept his new reality, despite the fact that he did not want to accept it. In the end, he had no choice. Over time, Richard came to adapt to his condition. He spoke with his doctor about minimizing his use of pain medication. He developed new interests to distract himself from his pain, and he joined a support group and helped others to deal with severe depression. He also began to walk, alone at first and then with his wife, as they began to mend their marriage.

Today Richard still has severe limitations, but he is no longer clinically depressed or anxious because he came to realize that he needed to accept his new reality. He made adaptations that allowed him to refocus on the future instead of the past, and he used his skills of speaking, listening, and cooperating to forge new coalitions. He increased his resources even though he was unable to reduce his needs. He found a new equilibrium based on a realistic and positive view of himself and his life.

Change happens. We cannot usually avoid change that catches us unaware. The kind of change that is very difficult for most of us is when we realize that we need to do something differently. One reason that people do not change, especially in relationships, is that they are afraid of the impact of their change on others.

> Amanda's husband, William, complained frequently and indelicately that she had gained too much weight and that she should go on a diet. Will even offered to go on walks with her as his contribution toward her efforts, and because he realized he could stand to lose a few pounds. Amanda decided to work on her weight. She began to eat healthier foods, she noticed and managed food portions, she went on walks (with and without Will), and she participated in a support group for individuals working on weight issues. Before long, Amanda's clothes began to fit better, she was able to get off certain medications, she started feeling better, and she began socializing much more often. Will became sullen and, at times, would angrily complain

that he was tired of eating salads and fruit. He wanted cheeseburgers and fries from the fast-food restaurant, food that he and Amanda used to enjoy. He began to get jealous that men seemed to be noticing Amanda and complained that she seemed to enjoy the attention too much. Marital conflict actually increased as Amanda's waist size decreased.

When individuals change, it affects others. We worry that if we change, our partner or others in our family will not be able to accept the changes or accept us. We worry that we will be rejected. As a result, we revert to older, more comfortable patterns of being. Sometimes, others attempt to get us to change back to the same old person that they are used to. Often a person working on weight reduction is confronted by others who push donuts and other goodies on the individual. The unconscious motivation may be, "If you change, I have to look at my life. I'm not ready to change." It seems easier to help the other individual return to old, unhealthy patterns than for us to change. Resistance to change comes from within and from without.

Despite our natural reluctance to change, change is happening all the time. We generally do not notice or document it, but it is happening all around us. The only certainty in life is change (and death and taxes). When individuals embrace change, they empower themselves to decide how they will be. Each of us is the product of our past, yet we do not have to be prisoners of that past. If the past contains good things, embrace them. If it reeks of foul experiences, it is still our past and it has shaped us to be who we are. We must embrace that reality and effect change by recognizing the need for change, making a decision to change, and then implementing attitudinal and behavioral changes that support the desired change. Individuals can then use the speaking, listening, and cooperating skills in the service of maintaining the change that was so hard to attain.

THE ASSESSMENT OF CHANGE: TOO LITTLE, TOO MUCH, TOO LATE

The problem with change is that we have to do something differently than we have always done. For this reason some people change very little. They think an old, dowdy, comfortable shoe is preferable to a new, shiny, stiff one. On the other hand, some people seem to change as frequently as they change clothes. Finally, some people come late to the party of change. Determining where a client is on the change continuum will assist the practitioner in developing appropriate treatment plans and intervention strategies.

Too Little

When assessing an individual's propensity to change, think of a rope on the floor, with one end representing people who change too little and the other end people who change constantly. Other words for the extremes on this continuum of change are rigid and chaotic.

Many people are inflexible. They have lived their lives a certain way and it would literally take an act of Congress to convince them to change. The dance is old and tired, but it is the dance they know. They doubt that they can change; they do not want to change; they cannot visualize the change; and they do not believe that they need to change.

When an individual fits this dynamic, the question of whether they will be able to change must be asked. The answer, for most people on this end of the continuum, is that change is extremely difficult and they will likely not change unless there is an overwhelming need to do so. Examples of an extreme need to change include: when a spouse threatens divorce, when a judge orders jail time, when health considerations demand it, or similar situations. Most of these people will be, either literally or figuratively, "court ordered" to change.

These individuals are good candidates for participation in psychotherapy, in that they have been shown the absolute need to change, or else. While change should occur because an individual wants it, sometimes change is inspired by a metaphorical sledgehammer. One caveat regarding this form of change is that individuals may initially have external motivations for change, but lasting change will occur only if individuals are able to internalize the need for change and see its value for themselves and, secondarily, for whoever demands that they change.

Identifying individuals on this end of the continuum is not difficult. They may be late for appointments, want to leave early, and frequently miss meetings. When the clinician asks for their goals, the response will normally be, "So-and-so thinks I need to change." The professional should also listen for phrases such as, "Yes, but . . ." These individuals are seen as being extremely rigid and, at first glance, appear unavailable for change. These people seem to speak up well but rarely listen.

The mental health professional must show these people the value to them of changing. Once they catch that vision—"What's in it for me?"—they will likely be able to codevelop treatment goals and agree to participation in intervention strategies. While this perspective may sound too egocentric and not the proper motivation for change, the fact is that most people only change when they are able to see its value for themselves.

Too Much

Some individuals change like the blowing wind. These individuals change like chameleons, based on the environment and on the people around them at any given point in time. They are on the extreme other end of the continuum. They change whenever it suits them. There is no consistency, no durability. These individuals are flexible to the point of being chaotic.

People who willingly change so often may not have a clear sense of who they are. They are classically unreliable. They are extremely susceptible to acquiescing to the needs of others. They likely do not know how to speak up for themselves yet are excellent listeners. They willingly change themselves to benefit others but at the cost of losing their identity.

In assessing these individuals, be aware of how easily they agree to make changes according to any recommendations made by others. Also evaluate how easily they adopt the clinician's perspective on any given topic. When individuals are able to change this much, they may not have a strong sense of self.

People who change a lot put themselves at risk of never being able to please the other people for whom they are changing. As a result, they are on a treadmill that never stops and actually increases in speed as the person becomes ever more anxious to please. These individuals ask others, "What do I have to do to please you?" Correct assessment of these individuals leads to treatment plans that will help them to clearly identify who they are and what they need, and will help them to speak up for those needs.

Too Late

Some individuals may not be aware of the need for change, may not hear other people's pleas that they change, may disagree about the need for change, may defer change, may look for a convenient time to change, or may wait until tomorrow and tomorrow never seems to come. All of these examples are people who want to change, or at least entertain the possibility for change, and who may or may not change soon enough to avoid catastrophic outcomes in their lives.

These individuals may be hard to assess correctly for a variety of reasons. When confronted with the need to change, after some argument, they may agree that change is necessary. They may even begin to make plans to change. Unfortunately, most of these people will delay change, will procrastinate, and will find other things to do that prevent immediate change. So, they say the right things but fail to follow through in a timely manner.

People with good intentions to change but terrible follow-through may be identified by how well they are able to make SMART goals. If they are able to be specific and make measurable, attainable, realistic, and time-limited goals, there is at least a chance that they will follow through. If they are vague about the change necessary, about the goal, about the start time, about how the change will occur, and about how and when the completion will occur, then the person likely falls into this category of failing to change in a timely manner. Questions that probe an individual's intent to change will likely produce information useful in deciding how quickly the person will likely change. Assessing these individuals is about listening to their stated intent to change and examining their plan for change.

These individuals may be good listeners and they may even talk a good game. The proof of their commitment to change is found in their ability to cooperate. The major question in cooperation is, "What are you willing to do in order to get what you want?" Some people want to change, in theory, yet find it really difficult in practice.

TREATMENT PLANS FOR CHANGE: WHAT I NEED, WHAT I WANT, WHAT I AM WILLING TO DO

Individuals who know how to change do not need treatment plans. Individuals with either rigid or chaotic responses to change need additional skills to provide for both flexibility and stability. A treatment plan for change provides a map that identifies both a destination and the different routes to get there. Such a plan will improve the individual's ability to embrace change and will provide the skills to handle change responsibly.

What I Need

An awareness of a need for change may come suddenly, as when a light bulb turns on and we realize with great clarity that change is necessary. More often, the awareness that change is needed comes more gradually, as in the changing of the seasons.

Others may recognize that we need to change before we see it. If we change solely because someone else wants us to, the change will likely be ephemeral and we may come to resent both the change and the person who highlighted our need to change.

What we almost always become aware of, even before we understand the need for change, is increasingly annoying stress in our lives. We may notice that we are having trouble sleeping or sleeping too much, that we cannot focus, that we cannot eat or that we eat too much; we may notice pain in the neck, shoulders, or back. We may also become irritable or develop gastrointestinal issues. We may notice that we are more depressed or anxious than before. Stress, in whatever form it manifests, is a signal that change is needed. When we pay attention to stress, we can determine if we need additional resources to deal with it or whether we need to make efforts to reduce it.

> Randy, the man who believed he was not an alcoholic until he was stopped by the police and cited for driving while intoxicated, had received many signals that a change was necessary before he ran into legal problems. Marital conflict had intensified over time and he was having erectile dysfunction on those few occasions when he and his wife engaged in sexual relations. He was irritable most of the time; he and his boss had almost come to blows on two occasions due to complaints about poor work performance. He was drinking more frequently after work, having blackouts on occasion, and finding that he could not go to sleep without having a beer or two (or more) to relax.
>
> Once Randy realized that he had problems, we began the treatment planning process by having him list a variety of issues he could work on in therapy. One issue, for example, was his alcoholism or, at least, problem-drinking. We also identified marital conflict, sexual dysfunction, anger management, and communication skills deficits as issues, and relaxation training as one method of resolving them.

The mental health professional can assist the client to determine what change is needed. When a client suggests several changes, the therapist will ask the client to pick just one option to work on. Picking one change is a way to help focus the client and will yield a greater likelihood of success. It is hard to solve many problems at once.

What I Want

What I want is not necessarily always what I need. I might want a new car, but I might also need to save money. I have to make a choice based on my priorities. If I make changes based only on what I want, I may overlook other necessary healthy changes.

Helping individuals differentiate between needs and wants is one of the ways that therapists can be helpful to clients. Providing a safe environment in which clients can discuss the stressors that they feel, the needs that they have, and the desires of their heart can allow clients to clarify their thinking and help them identify which choices for change they want to make and in what order.

Some clients do not know what they want. It is important to help clients decide what they want, help them to get very specific about their goals, and develop a treatment plan with them that identifies one goal for change that they want to pursue.

The process of problem solving for change involves identifying the problem, looking for the desired outcome, identifying a variety of changes that are possible to achieve the desired outcome, picking one change to make, and developing specific steps to make the goal a reality.

What I Am Willing to Do

No matter what changes have been identified as being necessary or desired, change will only occur if I make the efforts necessary to effect it. Therefore, the clinician must elicit from the client exactly what the client is willing to do in terms of time, energy, and effort.

> When I was an adolescent (not that long ago), I knew a teenage girl who was an amazing piano player. She was so good that I and several of her other friends would go to her house and sit in her living room for hours just to listen to her play. I used to muse about how wonderful it would be to learn to play the piano that well. I pondered the possibility of being invited to parties, where I would be asked to play for the adoring crowd. In my fantasy, girls would swoon at my skills. Unfortunately, I found out how she got to be so good at her craft: lots of practice. Since I was never willing to put the time into practicing the piano, I never became "the amazing piano guy." I think about that story whenever I ask clients to tell me what they are willing to do in order to get what they want. A treatment plan, no matter how well designed, will only work if the individual(s) involved commit to action, to doing something differently.

Often individuals will tell us what they are not willing to do. We must then ask them to identify what they are willing to do. Then, people are often vague about they will do. The clinician can help focus the individual on increasingly specific treatment goals. To the degree that the individual is able to be specific, there is a greater likelihood of success in making the desired change.

Journaling and making lists of desired changes can be a valuable exercise. The clinician has the opportunity to teach clients how to be specific about what they will do. It is important for clients to identify what they will do and when they will do it. The more people commit to change, the more likely that change will actually occur.

PRACTICAL INTERVENTIONS: LEARN FROM THE PAST, LIVE IN THE PRESENT, LOOK TOWARD THE FUTURE

Once a treatment plan has been developed, the clinician guides the client through activities or interventions that serve to help the client be successful in making the desired changes. Efforts at change are encouraged. Even unsuccessful efforts indicate that the client is actively involved in seeking a better future. That better future will likely be achieved more easily if the client learns from the past and lives in the present.

Learn From the Past

The past is the best predictor of the future. When individuals and families want to change, one place to look is toward the past. We look backward in order to avoid past errors, and also to remember past successes. Identifying the kinds of changes a family has gone through and how the family changed can be very instructional. First, it helps remind people that they have already been successful in making changes. Second, it helps them understand why it is important to make changes: the negative impact of stress before the change. Third, it reminds people to focus on one desired outcome. Fourth, it shows people that the specific steps we take affect whether change actually occurs. In that sense, looking toward the past and learning from it will encourage more changes in the present.

One way for individuals and families to learn from past accomplishments is to complete the Family Changes Worksheet (Figure 8.1). The following instructions will assist in completing this worksheet:

1. Identify changes that you or your family successfully completed in the recent past.

FIGURE 8.1
THE STEPS TO CHANGE (USED BY PERMISSION
OF FAMILY WELLNESS ASSOCIATES)

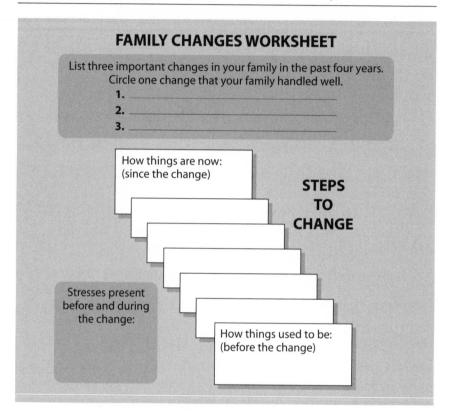

FAMILY CHANGES WORKSHEET

List three important changes in your family in the past four years.
Circle one change that your family handled well.

1. _____
2. _____
3. _____

How things are now:
(since the change)

**STEPS
TO
CHANGE**

Stresses present
before and during
the change:

How things used to be:
(before the change)

2. Circle which of those changes was particularly successful.
3. Write down how things were before the change.
4. Write down how things are now (since the change).
5. Write down the stressors present before and during the change.
6. Identify the steps that were necessary to make the change. Write them down in order from the bottom to the top, from the early changes to the later changes.

This exercise reminds individuals and families that they have already been successful in effecting prior changes. This can give them reason for hope that they can succeed in the changes that they are currently contemplating.

I received a letter recently, wherein Jocelyn described her journey since terminating psychotherapy three years ago. She described having finally decided to leave her abusive husband, after which she had moved to the mountains and healed from the emotional and physical abuse that she had endured. She reminded me that she had always loved art and that, during the course of therapy, she had been encouraged to pick one thing that she wanted to learn to do better. She had taken several art classes and was now proudly showing some of her paintings at local studios. Jocelyn said that focusing on changing one thing at a time had been helpful at a time in her life when she could not focus or concentrate on anything. She had found that attaining success in one small thing helped her to have hope that she could make some bigger changes. She closed the letter by saying that taking things one day and one moment at a time had literally saved her life: She had been suicidal when we worked together in therapy. There were many things she needed to change in her life. To attempt changing more than one thing at a time would have been impossible; it would have paralyzed her.

Looking back on successful changes reminds people that change is a step-by-step process that does not occur overnight. It is through carefully thinking about the many steps necessary to effect change, through planning the specific actions required, and by executing these steps in an appropriate order that goals can be achieved.

Live in the Present

We must learn from the past in order to avoid repeating the mistakes of the past. We can also learn from our successes in the past. We must, however, live in the present. It is in the present where change actually occurs. The past cannot be changed. The future is not yet available. It is only through living in the present that we can change the future.

In the present, we must pay attention to the signals that change is necessary. Once the therapist has elicited the stressors and the underlying changes that are required, he or she helps the client to identify potential areas for change and focuses the client on one specific change that will be worked on.

The changes will usually involve helping an individual learn to speak up more, speak less, listen more, listen less, cooperate more, or cooperate less. These are the skills that need to be utilized more or less in order to produce the changes that are required. Some changes require the assistance of others and some changes only require us to do something differently.

Look Toward the Future

Once we have learned from the past and are living in the present, we are in a great position to look forward toward the future. The clinician reminds clients that everyone makes mistakes and that it is the wise person who chooses to learn from mistakes. That wise person makes the changes necessary to be more successful. The person who chooses to make changes is actively creating the future. What may look like sudden fame or success in any field is usually preceded by years of effort in preparation for the opportunity for that so-called sudden fame. It is the hard work we do in the present that gives us the promise of a better tomorrow through the changes that we make, one step at a time.

SUMMARY

Nothing is as certain as change. The ability to withstand the vicissitudes of life, from birth to death, demands from humans the ability to adapt and to change. Some people are afraid of change; others embrace it. Some people change too little, while others change too much.

The Family Wellness practitioner assists people in appreciating the importance of change in our lives and finds ways to assist clients in developing goals for change that are congruent with the values of the individual in the present and for the future.

As we come to the end of this text on the Family Wellness model, I wish to provide an image that will allow mental health professionals to remember the cogent aspects of this way of helping people (see Figure 8.2). Family Wellness takes complex concepts and puts them into everyday language. Each person has two jobs: to be an individual and to connect with others. Each person needs three skills: speaking, listening, and cooperating. These skills form the foundation of a healthy individual and a healthy family. Healthy individuals and families exhibit three patterns: equal value and parents in charge, room to be close and apart, and expect change. When I conceptualize this model, I think of the Family Wellness House.